# Baking *with* Fortitude

BLOOMSBURY PUBLISHING
LONDON • OXFORD • NEW YORK • NEW DELHI • SYDNEY

Dedicated to my family

# Baking *with* Fortitude

Dee Rettali

# Contents

# Introduction

I named the bakehouse I founded in 2018 after the fortitude of people in kitchens, the steadfast craft of sourdough baking and the quality and character of the ingredients I choose to bake with.

Fortitude Bakehouse is the culmination of my early years growing up on the Munster Blackwater river in Ireland, watching my mother and grandmother bake, and then working in pioneering organic restaurants in London. When I was head baker at Bumblebee Natural Foods in 1995, it was miles ahead of its time with an emphasis on organic, biodynamic ingredients and a no-waste policy. I then went on to found Patisserie Organic, my first bakery. I met Jorge Fernandez when he asked me to create bakes for his coffee house, Fernandez & Wells, that would complement, not overwhelm, their coffees. For me, this meant creating bakes that allowed the flavour of the ingredients to shine – the fragrant notes of fruits and herbs, the aromatic warmth of spices and the tang of fermented butter, rather than a big hit of sweetness from sugary sponges and icing.

That is also why I started baking with a sourdough starter or fermented batter because I was searching for something you couldn't find in other bakeries or coffee houses. It's easy to use fashionable ingredients or techniques, but I wanted to create something with longevity. For me, baking is about crafting, where it's as much about the process as the end result. My motivation behind opening Fortitude was because I believed we could offer something that hadn't been done before, a product that was truly a new experience. Starters and ferments uniquely concentrate the flavours of ingredients, something my mother and grandmother used to do instinctively – steeping fruit in tea and then leaving it for a week before adding flour to make a fruit cake, for example. So I ferment my cake batter overnight or sometimes for up to three days to intensify and deepen the taste.

## The Craft of Baking

I see myself as a craft baker. To me, that means valuing the longstanding traditions of the baking I grew up with. I have never followed fads. For me, innovation comes from the inspiration within: it is about who you are – your provenance. Not that my grandmother would have used that word about herself or her ingredients. There wasn't a huge amount of choice in Ireland back then; it was more about selecting the best produce available and making the most of it. Nothing was added unnecessarily and nothing was wasted.

Within my baking, I combine traditional, quite old-fashioned methods with a modern approach. My method of fermenting a butter cake mixture is a new innovation in baking, but I do it to achieve the intensity of flavour that I remember from the bakes of my childhood. Though to be honest, my grandmother knew that sour milk made for a better soda bread so she would leave her milk on the windowsill until it started bubbling – it's a wonder that none of us got ill from it.

Longevity also has a second meaning for me. My bakes are created to last for days, even for up to a week. When I baked for Fernandez & Wells, they would want their cakes to keep for as long as possible so there would be less wastage at the cafés. Again, this need to reduce food waste comes out of both mine and Jorge's backgrounds. Our families kept cakes in tins, bringing them out every afternoon, but making each one last over the course of a week.

# What is a Cake?

I hope you'll be intrigued by the bakes you find in this book. They differ from the usual recipes found in other baking books, not just because of my fermentation process, but by how I define a 'cake'. When my grandmother made her white soda bread in a skillet over the fire, she called it 'sweet cake' – what made it sweet were the sultanas or apples or jam she added to it. I used to say to her that this was not a cake, but as it was something we ate in the afternoon for a treat, to her it was a cake. My mum used to add a jar of marmalade into the mixture, folding it into the soda bread dough before baking. When you toasted it the next day, you were basically eating toast and marmalade.

I call these kinds of bakes 'savoury cakes' – Jorge calls them 'bread-ish'. They are really enriched doughs, but without the laborious process. For example, is my brioche that is topped with sugar (see page 136) a bread or a cake? It's a bit of both really, while my banana and bilberry sourdough loaf cake (see page 164) is definitely more of a bread than a cake. American visitors to Fortitude see my bakes as bread because I bake them as loaves in loaf tins – a San Francisco baker who came especially to check out my bakes said that they were more like sweet bread than cake. But if you think about it, an Eccles cake (see page 114) is more tart than sweet and people have no problem eating that with cheese. For me, essentially, it's what we enjoyed as children – bakes that were heartwarming, familiar, satisfying, fortifying really, and made with a few honest ingredients. No fuss, no frills, no fancy decoration to hide behind. My customers tell me that the range of bakes on our counter reminds them of the cakes of their childhood, rather than what you see now in most shops.

## In this Book

Most of the chapters are centred around a base recipe with offshoots and variations. It was while I was creating recipes at Patisserie Organic, and then again at Fernandez & Wells and Fortitude, that I came up with the idea of making variations on the same base recipe to give five or six bakes that tasted so completely different that nobody realised they were all made from the same cake batter. So, once you've got the hang of the base mix, you'll be able to create something new each time and learn to suit your own taste or to use up whatever you have in the fridge or storecupboard.

Ultimately, this is artisan baking – but that term doesn't convey what it really is to be a commercial artisan baker (or any kind of crafter). You have to be slightly obsessive as well as courageous. There is hard work, long hours, kitchen politics and even moments of comedy in craft baking – the humanity of making things. That's what I want this book to show: the reality of baking, rather than picture-perfect bakes.

The first five chapters focus on my non-fermented bakes. The recipes can be made and baked straightaway and many are simple one-pot mixes. Some cake batters you can ferment overnight or leave for a few extra days to deepen the flavours – see the notes on fermenting in each recipe. There is no extra work for you if you choose to do this – you just need to plan that into your timings. These recipes are a good introduction to my baking methods and the fermented and starter-based recipes in the last chapter.

The recipes in the Herbs and Botanicals chapter are based on either a butter loaf cake mixture or one that uses olive oil instead of butter. The Fruit and Berries, Dairy, and Spices and Aromatics chapters focus on the ingredients I use most in my recipes – from my love of the farm and field and my relationship with Morocco. (My children are half Moroccan and we have spent a lot of time there.) Some of the Dairy recipes use fermented butter, which you'll find in the Storecupboard section (see page 178), along with my spice mixes and other fermented or preserved recipes. Bread-ish involves my soda bread batter, which is very thick and dry, like a bread, as well as my brioche base, a much more straightforward recipe to make than the traditional French version.

Chapter six is all about my sourdough cakes, which use a milk-based starter that you leave for a few days and is similar in some ways to a sourdough bread starter. The cake batters can be fermented (simply left to sit) too. This is the most technical chapter, but the cakes don't require a lot of work, just time and patience.

## Using Ingredients Well

This book is as much about understanding ingredients as understanding sourdough. I want to give you confidence in and a curiosity for the ingredients around us – the herbs, berries, spices, good butter and eggs, and molasses sugar, which all have an amazing depth of flavour. My butter cake (see page 156) is just butter, sugar, eggs, flour, and ground almonds, but the buttermilk starter gives it guts so you don't need to add anything more. Jorge grew up in a traditional Spanish family and, for them, cake means a simple sponge eaten after a meal with coffee. But the cake has such flavour – that's what inspired the butter cake.

As well as the more common grains, I bake with buckwheat, semolina and rye flours, along with olive oil, because they bring so much taste. Pomace oil, which is the second press from olives after extra-virgin oil has been made, is often considered a by-product. As you don't need the best press for bakes, put this otherwise discarded oil to good use.

My bakes are about pairing ingredients and then about pairing them with other foods too. Lavender goes well with pear – together they make each other taste better. I don't know why we need to search out new ingredients – new syrups, substitute products – when there's so much that's good and natural around us. I have such curiosity about what more I can do with the ingredients I already have – what I can do with the peel or the offcuts. I learned frugality from my grandmother, who got such flavour out of her few ingredients, so I know what potential that simplicity has.

My baking is also not about measuring or being precise. So many of my recipes have come out of accidents, like the fizzy apricots I use (see page 183), which happened when I left the cherries and apricots marinating in sugar and water for a week and they exploded. Or the fruit strap (see page 160) that came about when someone in my kitchen burned some really expensive organic dates and we had to find a way to revive them. Also a liquid batter is forgiving, so I want you to just get in there and give it a try. No one at Fortitude is a baker by training, but they all share a passion for crafting with their hands. By sharing my recipes and approach to baking, I want to take away the fear. Use your hands, get your fingers right into the bottom of the bowl and feel the dough. It's a craft – how does it feel to you?

## Baking for Wellbeing

As you will see, the nutritional side of baking is important to me – fortitude also represents having good health. Not just the benefits of fermenting but also choosing ingredients with the most nutritional value. But there is another aspect that is important to me and that is how it helps my mental wellbeing. The smell of herbs, fruit and spices always gives me a boost, the feel of the dough as I work it is almost meditative for me, the learning of a new craft and physical energy from hard work. And, of course, there's nothing like seeing the delight of my customers as they come in.

## Having Fortitude

Fortitude means many things: the longevity of craft baking traditions, the resolve of women who bake in professional kitchens or at home, the strength to speak out, the perseverance that Jorge sees in me. Jorge says when things go wrong, I take five minutes to let it sink in and then pick myself up. (I grew up in a family of eight, so no-one else was going to pick me up and I had to find my voice if I wanted to be heard.)

But I think that everyone has fortitude. For me, it's about our strength as a team. Working with empathy and generosity, sharing ideas and concerns, supporting each other. I came to London as an Irish immigrant in the 1980s and it was tough. I want to give people a chance at Fortitude. We're not a hippy commune or wholesome whole-food place, but I do see us as a co-operative.

We are nine altogether, with five core bakers, including myself. Rachid is the only one with baking experience and advises and organises the others. Sonia is from

Bolivia and does all the mixing; she's amazing. My daughter Soumiya is our front of house and does all the display and branding – she has a love of Korean branding from her Korean language studies. My other daughter Sophia set up our coffee section and my son Zakiyy has just started working at Fortitude too – he has been baking since he was tiny and both speaks and bakes Japanese. Deivey is our pot washer. And Jorge is my founding partner and has been fundamental to Fortitude's success. He designed Fortitude, spending days finding the right blue and introducing our wooden counter, which everyone remembers about the bakehouse.

Those early days were such hard work, I remember, because it was just the two of us baking, Irma (one of the original bakers) and me. Every so often we would have to go and sit outside for a while, just to have a break, and then we'd pull ourselves together, pick ourselves up and go back inside. As I write this now, as COVID is changing our lives, it feels as if we're going through another such time. I carry responsibility for my staff, and so we are finding ways to carry on, but we need fortitude once more.

## A Few Notes on Ingredients

*Flour*
I believe good bread is the result not just of the sourdough fermentation process but also from using the best organic flour made from heritage grains as well as the quality of the milling, which should ideally be stoneground. I urge you to use the best ingredients you can.

*Fruits and vegetables*
I learned from my parents and my time at Bumblebee that you don't waste anything and so, when it comes to fresh produce, I don't worry about shape or size. Fruits and vegetables don't have to be perfect and they have no use-by date.

*Butter*
All butter is salted, unless otherwise stated. This works better for me than adding salt to the recipe and it takes away some of the sweetness.

*Eggs*
All eggs are medium, unless otherwise stated. It is also important to use the best eggs you can find. I use St. Ewè eggs that have yolks as yellow as a sunflower – it makes the butter cakes look even more buttery, and the fat in egg yolks is very good for cakes.

# Herbs *and* Botanicals

My love of herbs, berries and other botanicals stems from my childhood. My mother is an incredible grower and we had access to so much fresh seasonal produce both in our garden and on our doorstep. We used to forage for elderberries and elderflowers in the fields around us. While working for Bumblebee Natural Foods, I learned the principles of using specific ingredients within baking, such as raw wildflower honey and Bach Flower Remedies, to promote health. When I started baking professionally, I wanted to create bakes that would sit happily alongside teas and coffees, complementing their robust flavours. Most cakes rely on sugar, but I realised that through the fermentation process I could give herbs, fruit and spices a deeper, more intense taste. I tend to pair fruit and herbs together – apricots with thyme, for example – to contrast the floral notes of fresh fruits with the bitter hints of the herbs. When you chop herbs, they release their oils that will infuse a cake batter while it ferments – the fragrance of the fermenting batter when you open the lid of the tub is amazing, one of those quiet moments for the baker to savour. Pastry chefs are traditionally limited to a much smaller range of ingredients than savoury chefs; perhaps I have always envied those chefs and wanted to bring a breadth of flavours to my baking.

There are two base cake recipes in this chapter: a butter base mix and an olive oil base mix. Each cake batter can be mixed up and baked straightaway, but as you will see at the beginning of each section, these cake batters can also be fermented. I strongly recommend that you leave the olive oil cake batter to ferment at least overnight in the fridge before baking. The butter for the butter base cake batter can also be left to ferment for 2–3 days at room temperature. Fermenting a batter gives the cake an incredible intensity of flavour as the fruit has time to come alive as the mixture becomes oilier; this gives the batter longevity – it will keep for a week, if uncut – as well as a thicker, denser texture. Fermenting the mixture also helps to break down the sugars and makes the cake more digestible.

The olive oil base mix comes from my time working at Bumblebee in the late eighties when I wanted to create an alternative to butter-based cakes. While many countries have a tradition of making cakes with olive oil, I'm pretty sure that I was the first in London. It came out of my interest in health, which of course is what Bumblebee and the organic movement is founded on. Olive oil is all about the good fats and makes a lovely moist cake, which also lasts. I didn't want to use coconut oil because it has such a strong flavour and the same goes for extra-virgin olive oil, so that is why I use pomace oil. Made from the second press of olives, after the extra-virgin oil is extracted, pomace oil has a less strong flavour than oil from the first press. Because there is less demand for pomace oil, a lot of it is thrown away, but I have always believed that there should be no food waste of any kind in the kitchen. Pomace oil also works really well with alternative flours, such as polenta and semolina – again something inspired by the gluten-free cooking at Bumblebee. If you have trouble sourcing pomace oil, you can use light virgin olive oil (not extra-virgin) in its place.

I use dark muscovado sugar when I need a strong flavour to work with other powerful ingredients and unrefined golden caster sugar when paired with lighter flavours. The muscovado sugar works really well with fruit with high acidity, such as bananas and pineapple, and stabilises fermented cakes: white sugars just turn to liquid.

All the herbs I use come either from The Organic Herb Trading Company or Michael Isted (The Herball) with whom I collaborated on a botanical cake collection a few years ago. Michael also forages all the herbs used in our bespoke tea blends at Fortitude. The Tulsi mix is made exclusively for us: Michael asked me how I would reflect my personality in a tea, which I found very difficult to answer, so he decided it should be mellow yet fresh, with the flavours you would find in the hedgerow alongside cinnamon to represent the amber of the Moroccan souks.

Finally, I have much to thank Suzanne Sharp from Canada for. Many years ago, she was making vegan and gluten-free food and taught me about vegan cooking (I went on to make vegan birthday cakes for Prince Charles, Madonna and Damon Albarn, among others). It was so new then, but my only aim was to make vegan and gluten-free bakes taste as good as 'normal' cakes. Those recipes are still amazing. Many of our bakes at Fortitude are vegan, including the ever-popular Chocolate and Blackberry Loaf Cake (see page 61), but you wouldn't know.

Herbs and Botanicals

# Butter Loaf Cake Base Mix

All the butter base mixes taste wonderful when baked immediately, but I would nudge you in favour of keeping them for 2–3 days in an airtight container in a cool place (but not in the fridge).

I often let these mixes stand for a few days before I use them, which means that each loaf has a different flavour profile, all clearly defined – the tea brews, the fruit fizzes and ferments and the herbs and botanicals soften.

To ferment the butter, I leave it to soften out of the fridge for 2 days because I find it gives a very oily, powerful buttery flavour to the cakes.

# Meadowsweet *and* Honey Butter Loaf Cake

As a homage to my mother, who is the greenest-fingered human
I know, I wanted to create a cake with the flavours of our garden in
the summertime. Our house was always full of the sweet, woody scent
of geraniums; the outside heady with the smell of freshly cut grass.
To me, meadowsweet tastes of summer flowers on a warm rainy day
and, paired with wildflower honey, it evokes memories of a garden.
Do use meadowsweet only in moderation, though. To give this cake its
particular texture and flavour, it needs to be left overnight in the fridge
so the honey can set – it will taste almost like a nougat found in Morocco.

**Makes 1 loaf cake**

- 900-g/2-lb loaf tin, lined
  with baking parchment

250g salted butter, softened
  (see note on fermenting)
250g unrefined golden
  caster sugar
4 eggs
200g organic self-raising
  white flour
½ teaspoon baking powder
100g ground almonds
100ml buttermilk
  (see page 180)
½ teaspoon dried
  meadowsweet
150g raw wildflower honey
Butter and fine sea salt,
  to serve

Preheat the oven to 200°C/Fan 180°C/Gas 6.

In a large bowl, cream together the butter and sugar
using an electric whisk until light and fluffy. Add the
eggs, one at a time and continue to mix until combined,
but do not overmix.

In a separate bowl, sift together the flour and baking
powder, then add the ground almonds.

Fold the flour and almond mixture into the creamed
butter using a metal spoon. Gradually add the
buttermilk and then, when it is almost combined,
add the meadowsweet. Gently fold the meadowsweet
through, making sure every bit of the cake batter
contains herbs.

Pour the cake batter into the lined loaf tin, level the
surface and tap the tin sharply on the work surface to
release any trapped air pockets. Bake in the centre of
the hot oven for 50 minutes or until it springs back
to the touch.

Once the cake is baked, warm the honey in a small pan
over a low heat. While the cake is hot and still in the tin,
prick the top using a fork or skewer and pour over the
warm honey.

Leave the cake in the tin until it's completely cool, then cover and place in the fridge overnight so that the honey soaks the cake and sets.

When ready to serve, remove the cake from the fridge and let it stand for a few minutes. Cut the cake into thick slices, spread them with butter and sprinkle over a pinch of fine sea salt.

When stored in an airtight container, this loaf cake will keep for 7 days.

TO FERMENT
Store the cake batter in an airtight container in a cool room (not in the fridge) for 2 days to allow the mixture to ferment. You can also leave the butter out of the fridge for 2 days to soften and ferment slightly (see note on page 16).

# Sage, Buttermilk *and* Almond Butter Loaf Cake

This is a cake I created for Michael Isted, a herbalist who forages the herbs we use in the teas served at Fortitude. Michael uses hemp in his teas, which makes them slightly tart, and so he wanted a cake that was savoury rather than overly sweet.

**Makes 1 loaf cake**

- 900-g/2-lb loaf tin, lined with baking parchment

250g salted butter, softened (see note on fermenting)

250g unrefined golden caster sugar

4 eggs

200g organic self-raising white flour

½ teaspoon baking powder

100g ground almonds

100ml buttermilk (see page 180)

100g almonds, skinned and chopped

1 tablespoon finely chopped fresh sage leaves

1 tablespoon flaked almonds

Preheat the oven to 200°C/Fan 180°C/Gas 6.

In a large bowl, cream together the butter and sugar using an electric whisk until light and fluffy. Add the eggs one at a time and continue to mix until combined, but do not overmix.

In a separate bowl, sift together the flour and baking powder, then add the ground almonds.

Fold the flour and almond mixture into the creamed butter using a metal spoon. Gradually add the buttermilk and then, when it is almost combined, add the chopped almonds and sage. Gently fold the nuts and herbs through the cake batter so they are evenly distributed.

Pour the cake batter into the lined loaf tin and sprinkle over the flaked almonds. Bake in the centre of the hot oven for 50 minutes or until it springs back to the touch.

Leave the cake in the tin to cool for at least 1 hour until set and there is no more steam.

When stored in an airtight container, this loaf cake will keep for 7 days.

TO FERMENT
Store the cake batter in an airtight container in a cool place (not in the fridge) for 2 days to allow the mixture to ferment. You can also leave the butter out of the fridge for 2 days to soften and ferment slightly.

*From left to right:* Sage, Buttermilk and Almond Butter Loaf Cake, Earl Grey Tea and Lemon Butter Loaf Cake, Rosemary and Plum Butter Loaf Cake, Thyme and Apricot Butter Loaf Cake.

Herbs and Botanicals

# Rosemary *and* Plum Butter Loaf Cake

Over a decade ago, when I started to work with coffee specialists Fernandez & Wells, Jorge Fernandez asked me to create a series of cakes to complement their coffee during tasting sessions. This is the first cake I devised to that brief – the rosemary baked into the loaf works beautifully well after a sip of espresso. I decorate this cake either with a sugar-dusted, crystallised sprig of rosemary (something we used to do as kids) or scattered with fresh plum pieces.

**Makes 1 loaf cake**

- 900-g/2-lb loaf tin, lined with baking parchment

250g salted butter, softened
   (see note on fermenting)
250g dark muscovado sugar
4 eggs
200g organic self-raising
   white flour
½ teaspoon baking powder
50g ground almonds
100ml buttermilk
   (see page 180)
150g fresh ripe plums, stoned
   and finely chopped
1 tablespoon freshly chopped
   rosemary leaves
Plum jam, to glaze

**To decorate**
50g fresh ripe plums, stoned
   and roughly chopped, or
   a large rosemary sprig,
   crystallised

Preheat the oven to 200°C/Fan 180°C/Gas 6.

In a large bowl, cream together the butter and sugar using an electric whisk until light and fluffy. Add the eggs one at a time and continue to mix until combined, but do not overmix.

In a separate bowl, sift together the flour and baking powder, then add the ground almonds.

Fold the flour mixture into the creamed butter using a metal spoon. Gradually add the buttermilk and, when almost combined, add the finely chopped plums and rosemary leaves. Gently fold the fruit and herbs through the cake batter so they are evenly distributed.

Pour the cake batter into the lined loaf tin. Bake in the centre of the hot oven for 50 minutes or until it springs back to the touch.

Warm the jam in a small pan over a low heat. While the cake is still hot and in the tin, glaze the top of the loaf with the warm jam. Leave the cake in the tin to cool for at least 1 hour until set and there is no more steam.

Before serving, remove the cake from the tin and decorate the top with plum pieces or a rosemary sprig.

When stored in an airtight container, this loaf cake will keep for 7 days.

Store the cake batter in an airtight container in a cool place (not in the fridge) for 2 days to allow the mixture to ferment. You can also leave the butter out of the fridge for 2 days to soften and ferment slightly.

Herbs and Botanicals

# Lavender *and* Pear Butter Loaf Cake

I developed this cake during my time working with Fernandez & Wells, and I still bake it today. A hint of lavender complements milky coffees. At that time, not many people got my kind of baking, but Jorge Fernandez and his customers understood that quality ingredients with good provenance offer better flavours than sugary syrups and frostings. This gave me free rein to work with herbs, spices and other botanicals.

**Makes 1 loaf cake**

- 900-g/2-lb loaf tin, lined with baking parchment

250g salted butter, softened (see note on fermenting)
250g unrefined golden caster sugar
4 eggs
200g organic self-raising white flour
½ teaspoon baking powder
50g ground almonds
100ml buttermilk (see page 180)
125g fresh ripe pears, chopped into 1-cm /½-inch pieces (no need to peel if organic)
1 teaspoon dried lavender, plus extra to decorate
Apricot jam, to glaze

Preheat the oven to 200°C/Fan 180°C/Gas 6.

In a bowl, cream together the butter and sugar using an electric whisk until light and fluffy. Add the eggs one at a time and mix until combined, but do not overmix.

In a separate bowl, sift together the flour and baking powder, then add the ground almonds.

Fold the flour and almonds into the creamed butter mix using a metal spoon. Gradually add the buttermilk and then, when it is almost combined, add the chopped pear and lavender. Gently fold the fruit and herbs through the cake batter until evenly distributed.

Pour the cake batter into the lined loaf tin. Bake for 50 minutes or until it springs back to the touch.

Warm the jam in a small pan over a low heat. While the cake is still hot and in the tin, glaze the top of the loaf with the warm jam. Leave the cake in the tin to cool for at least 1 hour until set and there is no more steam. Before serving, scatter over a few dried lavender flowers.

When stored in an airtight container, this loaf cake will keep for 7 days.

TO FERMENT
Store the cake batter in an airtight container in a cool place (not the fridge) for 2 days to ferment. You can also leave the butter out of the fridge for 2 days to ferment.

# Thyme *and* Apricot Butter Loaf Cake

I use fermented fizzy apricots for this cake at the bakery, which gives the bake a bit of a pop, but fresh apricots are also great when they are in season.

**Makes 1 loaf cake**

- 900-g/2-lb loaf tin, lined with baking parchment

250g salted butter, softened (see note on fermenting)
250g dark muscovado sugar
4 eggs
200g organic self-raising white flour
½ teaspoon baking powder
50g ground almonds
100ml buttermilk (see page 180)
150g fresh or fizzy apricots (see page 183), stoned and finely chopped
½ tablespoon freshly chopped thyme leaves
25g flaked almonds (optional)
Apricot jam, to glaze

Preheat the oven to 200°C/Fan 180°C/Gas 6.

In a large bowl, cream together the butter and sugar using an electric whisk until light and fluffy. Add the eggs one at a time and continue to mix until combined, but do not overmix.

In a separate bowl, sift together the flour and baking powder, then add the ground almonds.

Fold the flour and almond mixture into the creamed butter using a metal spoon. Gradually add the buttermilk and then, when it is almost combined, add the chopped apricots and thyme. Gently fold the fruit and herbs through the cake batter so they are evenly distributed.

Pour the cake batter into the lined loaf tin. Scatter the flaked almonds across the top, if using. Bake in the centre of the hot oven for 50 minutes or until it springs back to the touch.

Warm the jam in a small pan over a low heat. While the cake is still hot and in the tin, glaze the top of the loaf with the warm jam. Leave the cake in the tin to cool for at least 1 hour until set and there is no more steam.

When stored in an airtight container, this loaf cake will keep for 7 days.

TO FERMENT
Before you scatter over the almonds, store the cake batter in an airtight container in a cool place (not in the fridge) for 2 days to ferment. You can also leave the butter out of the fridge for 2 days to soften and ferment slightly.

# Earl Grey Tea *and*
# Lemon Butter Loaf Cake

The teas from Tim at Postcard Teas, whom Fernandez & Wells used to do pairings and tastings with, are on a different dimension to any other teas and offer this cake a wonderful fragrance as well as taste.

**Makes 1 loaf cake**

• 900-g/2-lb loaf tin, lined with baking parchment

2 tablespoons loose-leaf Earl Grey tea

Zest and juice of 3 organic, unwaxed lemons

250g salted butter, softened (see note on fermenting)

250g dark muscovado sugar

4 eggs

200g organic self-raising white flour

½ teaspoon baking powder

50g ground almonds

100ml buttermilk (see page 180)

Place the tea in a shallow dish with the lemon zest and juice. Leave for 1 hour at room temperature.

Preheat the oven to 200°C/Fan 180°C/Gas 6.

In a bowl, cream together the butter and sugar using an electric whisk until light and fluffy. Add the eggs one at a time and mix until combined, but do not overmix.

In a separate bowl, sift together the flour and baking powder, then add the ground almonds.

Fold the flour and almonds into the creamed butter using a metal spoon. Gradually add the buttermilk and then, when almost combined, add the tea and lemon. Gently fold the tea and lemon zest through the cake batter until evenly distributed.

Pour the cake batter into the lined loaf tin. Bake in the centre of the hot oven for 50 minutes or until it springs back to the touch.

Leave the cake in the tin to cool for at least 1 hour until set and there is no more steam.

When stored in an airtight container, this loaf cake will keep for 7 days.

TO FERMENT
Store the cake batter in an airtight container in a cool place (not in the fridge) for 2 days to ferment. You can also leave the butter out of the fridge for 2 days to soften and ferment slightly.

# Basil *and* Strawberry Butter Loaf Cake

Instead of the usual ground almonds, I use coconut flour in this butter loaf cake mixture as it works really nicely with the basil and strawberries. As coconut flour is super absorbent, this cake has a more pudding-like texture. If you prefer, you can use ground almonds.

**Makes 1 loaf cake**

- 900-g/2-lb loaf tin, lined with baking parchment

250g salted butter, softened (see note on fermenting)

250g unrefined golden caster sugar

4 eggs

200g organic self-raising white flour

50g coconut flour

½ teaspoon baking powder

100ml buttermilk (see page 180)

125g fresh ripe strawberries, hulled and halved

2 tablespoons roughly torn fresh basil leaves, plus extra to serve

Strawberries in syrup, to serve

Preheat the oven to 200°C/Fan 180°C/Gas 6.

In a large bowl, cream together the butter and sugar using an electric whisk until light and fluffy. Add the eggs one at a time and continue to mix until combined, but do not overmix.

In a separate bowl, sift together the flour, coconut flour and baking powder.

Fold the flour mixture into the creamed butter using a metal spoon. Gradually add the buttermilk and then, when it is almost combined, add the strawberries and basil. Gently fold the fruit and herbs through the cake batter so they are evenly distributed.

Pour the cake batter into the lined loaf tin. Bake in the centre of the hot oven for 50 minutes or until it springs back to the touch. Leave the cake in the tin to cool for at least 1 hour until set and there is no more steam.

Serve thick slices of the cake, accompanied by strawberries in syrup and scattered with basil leaves.

When stored in an airtight container, this loaf cake will keep for 7 days.

TO FERMENT
Store the cake batter in an airtight container in a cool place (not in the fridge) for 2 days to allow the mixture to ferment. You can also leave the butter out of the fridge for 2 days to soften and ferment slightly.

# Tarragon *and* Apple Syrup Butter Loaf Cake

I love to mix up flavours in cakes with unusual pairings of fruits, herbs and spices. As a countrywoman who has found herself in the city, I yearn for the outdoors, for the grasses, flowers and herbs, and so I bring them into my cakes whenever I bake to feel connected to nature.

**Makes 1 loaf cake**

• 900-g/2-lb loaf tin, lined
  with baking parchment

150g cooking apples (about
  2 apples), peeled and chopped
  into 2.5-cm/1-inch cubes
250g salted butter, softened
  (see note on fermenting)
250g unrefined golden
  caster sugar
4 eggs
200g organic self-raising
  white flour
½ teaspoon baking powder
100g ground almonds
100ml buttermilk
  (see page 180)
1 tablespoon finely chopped
  fresh tarragon leaves
4 apples, juiced (or
  a good-quality juice,
  like Chegworth Valley's
  Cox and Bramley Juice)
6 tablespoons soft brown
  sugar

Cook the apples in a large pan over a medium heat for 15 minutes or until almost cooked down. Leave to cool.

Preheat the oven to 200°C/Fan 180°C/Gas 6.

In a bowl, cream together the butter and caster sugar using an electric whisk until light and fluffy. Add the eggs one at a time and mix until combined, but do not overmix.

In a separate bowl, sift together the flour and baking powder, then add the ground almonds.

Fold the flour mixture into the creamed butter using a metal spoon. Gradually add the buttermilk and then, when it is almost combined, add the cooked apples and chopped tarragon. Gently fold the fruit and herbs through the cake batter so it is evenly distributed.

Pour the cake batter into the lined loaf tin. Bake for 50 minutes or until it springs back to the touch.

To make the syrup, warm the apple juice and brown sugar in a pan over a high heat for 8 minutes or until the sugar melts and the syrup bubbles. While the cake is hot and still in the tin, prick the top using a fork or skewer and pour over the warm apple syrup. Leave the cake in the tin until it's completely cool. Either cover the cake and place it in the fridge overnight so the syrup sets, or serve the cake straightaway, cut into thick slices and with custard poured over the top.

When stored in an airtight container, this loaf cake will keep for 7 days.

Once mixed, store the cake batter in an airtight container in a cool place (not in the fridge) for 2 days to allow the mixture to ferment. You can also leave the butter out of the fridge for 2 days to ferment slightly.

# Olive Oil Base Mix

I use pomace oil in many of my cake recipes because it has a less overwhelming flavour than extra-virgin olive oil, and because it's less in demand it's often cheaper. The pomace oil we use in the bakehouse comes from Odysea Foods. You'll be able to source it online but if you can't find it, light virgin olive oil will be fine (but not extra-virgin because its flavour is too powerful).

TO FERMENT THE BASE MIX

You can bake this immediately, but I always leave it at least overnight in the fridge – you can leave the olive oil mix for up to 3 days in the fridge. The oil acts as a preserving agent, but it will separate – the dense liquid rises to the top, so you just need to fold it all together to combine again. The basic mix is eggs, sugar, polenta and olive oil with citrus as the activator – banana doesn't work here.

Herbs and Botanicals

*From left to right:* Bilberry and Lemon Olive Oil Loaf Cake, Elderflower and Orange Olive Oil Loaf Cake.

Herbs and Botanicals

# Elderflower *and* Orange Olive Oil Loaf Cake

Back home in Ireland, we didn't cook with elderflower or even use it to make cordial. It was something only cows chewed on in hedgerows. When I arrived in London, I found it funny that people used elderflower as an ingredient. Now I do too, foraged by Michael Isted of The Organic Herb Trading Company. This pairing with fresh oranges works very well.

**Makes 1 loaf cake**

- 900-g/2-lb loaf tin, lined with baking parchment

170ml pomace oil (or light virgin olive oil)
200g unrefined golden caster sugar
4 eggs
125g fine ground polenta (not instant)
200g ground almonds
1½ teaspoons baking powder
Zest and juice of 2 organic, unwaxed oranges
2 teaspoons dried elderflowers, crushed
Icing sugar, to dust
Orange segments, peeled, to decorate

In a large bowl, beat together the pomace oil and sugar with an electric whisk until light and fluffy. Add the eggs one at a time and continue to mix until combined, but do not overmix.

In a separate bowl, combine the polenta, ground almonds and baking powder.

Fold the polenta and almonds into the whipped olive oil using a metal spoon. When it is almost combined, add the orange zest and juice and the elderflowers. Gently fold the zest and flowers through the cake batter until evenly distributed. Leave overnight in the fridge.

Preheat the oven to 200°C/Fan 180°C/Gas 6.

Fold any oil that is sitting on the surface back into the mixture to combine again. Pour the cake batter into the lined tin and place it on a baking tray. Bake in the centre of the hot oven for 50 minutes or until it springs back to the touch. Leave the cake in the tin to cool completely.

Before serving, dust with icing sugar and arrange orange segments on the top of the cake.

When stored in an airtight container in the fridge, this loaf cake will keep for 7 days.

TO FERMENT
Store the cake batter in an airtight container in the fridge for up to 3 days to allow it to ferment. Fold any oil sitting on the surface back into the mixture before baking.

# Bilberry *and* Lemon Olive Oil Loaf Cake

Bilberries remind me of when we used to fraughan – or forage – back in Ireland, so I was delighted to find frozen organic bilberries from Lithuania. We use them in our cakes at Fortitude. Bilberries have an incredible colour and make the cake looks as if it is leaking ink. If you can't find bilberries, you can use blueberries.

**Makes 1 loaf cake**

- 900-g/2-lb loaf tin, lined with baking parchment

170ml pomace oil (or light virgin olive oil)
200g unrefined golden caster sugar
4 eggs
125g fine ground polenta (not instant)
200g ground almonds
1½ teaspoons baking powder
Zest and juice of 2 organic, unwaxed lemons
100g bilberries or blueberries, crushed
Extra berries, to decorate

In a large bowl, beat together the pomace oil and sugar with an electric whisk until light and fluffy. Add the eggs one at a time and continue to mix until combined, but do not overmix.

In a separate bowl, combine the polenta, ground almonds and baking powder.

Fold the polenta and almond mixture into the whipped olive oil using a metal spoon. When it is almost combined, add the lemon zest and juice and the crushed bilberries. Gently fold the zest and berries through the cake batter so they are evenly distributed. Leave overnight in the fridge.

Preheat the oven to 200°C/Fan 180°C/Gas 6.

Fold any oil that is sitting on the surface back into the mixture to combine again. Pour the cake batter into the lined tin and place it on a baking tray. Dot the surface of the cake with extra berries. Bake in the centre of the hot oven for 50 minutes or until it springs back to the touch. Leave the cake in the tin to cool completely.

When stored in an airtight container in the fridge, this cake will keep for 7 days.

TO FERMENT
Store the cake batter in an airtight container in the fridge for up to 3 days to allow it to ferment. Fold any oil sitting on the surface back into the mixture before baking.

# Rose *and* Pistachio Little Buns

At Fortitude, I top these rosewater-flavoured buns with organic dried rose buds from the Merzouga valley in Morocco. I have visited this region on many occasions, where you are always greeted by the heady floral smell of organic roses.

**Makes 12 little buns**

• 12-hole muffin tin or easy-release silicone mould, greased well with oil

170ml pomace oil (or light virgin olive oil)
200g unrefined golden caster sugar
4 eggs
125g fine semolina
50g pistachios, finely ground into a flour
200g ground almonds
1½ teaspoons baking powder
25ml rosewater

**To decorate**
250g icing sugar
25g finely chopped pistachios
12 dried rose buds (optional)

In a large bowl, beat together the pomace oil and caster sugar with an electric whisk until light and fluffy. Add the eggs one at a time and continue to mix until combined, but do not overmix.

In a separate bowl, combine the semolina, ground pistachios, ground almonds and baking powder.

Fold the semolina mixture into the whipped olive oil mix using a metal spoon. When it is almost combined, add the rosewater and gently fold through. Leave overnight in the fridge.

Preheat the oven to 200°C/Fan 180°C/Gas 6.

Fold any oil that is sitting on the surface back into the mixture to combine again. Making sure that the muffin tin or mould is greased well with oil, divide the mixture equally between the holes of the tin or mould, then place it on a baking tray. Bake in the centre of the hot oven for 22 minutes or until the buns feel set to the touch.

Transfer the buns from the tin or mould to a wire cooling rack and leave to cool completely.

To make the icing, mix the icing sugar with just enough warm water to make a thick paste. Spread the top of each bun with the icing using the back of a spoon and sprinkle over the pistachios. If preferred, place a dried rose bud in the middle of each bun.

When stored in an airtight container in the fridge, these little buns will keep for 7 days.

Once mixed, store the cake batter in an airtight container in the fridge for up to 3 days to allow it to ferment. Fold any oil sitting on the surface back into the mixture before baking.

# Thyme *and* Lemon Basbousa Buns

I started making these little buns at Fernandez & Wells to complement an espresso. A cross between a cake batter and a dough, and a little like baklava because it's soaked in syrup, basbousa is made widely across the Middle East in many different ways, but always using semolina. This recipe is also a nod to my childhood in Ireland where we ate baked semolina pudding – I make it now because I like to use less-common grains. You can make the syrup the night before and use it to add extra stickiness to sticky buns – it keeps for weeks in the fridge.

**Makes 12 little buns**

- 12-hole muffin tin or easy-release silicone mould, greased well with melted butter

500g fine semolina
175g ground almonds
60g unrefined golden caster sugar
2½ teaspoons bicarbonate of soda
130g unsalted butter, melted, plus extra for greasing
300ml buttermilk (see page 180)

**For the syrup**
250g unrefined golden caster sugar
3 fresh thyme sprigs
300ml cold water
1 tablespoon orange flower water

Preheat the oven to 200°C/Fan 180°C/Gas 6.

First, make the syrup. Combine all the ingredients in a pan and simmer over a low heat for 10 minutes or until the syrup starts to look glossy. Set aside to cool for at least 30 minutes.

Meanwhile, make the buns. In a large bowl, combine the semolina, ground almonds, caster sugar and bicarbonate of soda. Add the melted butter and buttermilk and mix until well combined using a metal spoon. The mixture will seem stiff but that is how it is meant to be.

Making sure that the tray is well greased, press 100g of the mixture into each hole of the muffin tin or mould, then place it on a baking tray. Bake in the centre of the hot oven for 25 minutes or until the buns feel set to the touch – you don't want them to turn golden brown.

Pass the cooled syrup through a sieve to remove the thyme. While the buns are still hot, transfer them from the tin or mould to a dish, packing them in tightly, and pour the syrup over. Leave the buns in the dish until the syrup has been absorbed. Chill the buns for 1 hour in the fridge before eating.

When stored in an airtight container in the fridge, these little buns will keep for up to 5 days.

# Fruit *and* Berries

Fruit is incredibly sensory – its smell and feel when you're choosing
what to buy and then again when you eat the fruit – and evokes a
memory in everyone. For me, fruit has to be seasonal to be at its best:
lemons through winter and blood oranges in January bring sunshine
to the kitchen when there is little other colour, and then berries,
especially blackberries, through the summer and autumn months.
I remember my grandmother taking my sisters and me out to pick
blackberries in September and October. In a single day, we would fill
buckets with blackberries. Granny said they were for us to eat, but
really she was selling them to local jam makers in an early version
of a sustainable, circular economy. That was when I learned to see
potential in everything around me.

Tinned fruit was considered a treat when I was growing up. My
grandmother ran a cannery in the early fifties (remarkable in a time
when women didn't work) and she would take her two girls to the
factory on her bike. We were allowed tinned peaches with cream on
a Sunday afternoon; it was a great means of enjoying fruit – peaches,
pears, strawberries – whatever the season. Being able to enjoy
favourite fruits all year round is another reason to preserve them
in whatever way you like.

My time at Bumblebee also taught me to value the health benefits
of eating fruit, both for the body and the mind. I think citrus fruits
and berries are really beneficial. My grandmother used to drink aloe
vera juice and make gooseberry jam because she considered them good
for the brain – this was 20 years ago of course, so she was way ahead
of her time. In Morocco I saw how they believe that oranges are good
for your brain and heart – they use orange oil in food and to refresh
yourself and the house.

The first set of recipes in this chapter, my one-bowl yogurt cakes,
follow a base recipe that is similar to the butter base mix in the Herbs
and Botanicals chapter (see pages 16–31), but with less process.
Everything goes into a single bowl, which you can either leave to
ferment naturally to intensify the flavours or bake right away. If you
bake the mixture immediately, it will be less oily than a fermented
batter and result in a cake similar to a Madeira but with a good
structure so you can add lots of different kinds of fruit to it. I know

bakers do various things to stop the fruit from dropping down to the bottom of the cake while in the oven, but I simply pour the batter into the tin, scatter the fruit on top and then swirl it in with a spoon.

While the one-bowl cakes share the same base mix, each little bun recipe uses a different base mix – the only thing they have in common is their shape. We started making little buns at Fortitude because people often want just something small to snack on, but I always pack as much flavour and goodness into them as possible – fruit is the perfect filling. Three of the little bun recipes that follow are gluten-free and one is vegan.

If you want to finish your bake nicely, you can brush it with some apricot jam. I've always loved a glaze – I think it's the pastry chef in me – as it makes a bake pop. We always keep a stock of jam at Fortitude. Apricot jam works best for a glaze as it is less sweet than strawberry and raspberry jams and because it has a more neutral colour that gives a golden sheen to a cake. I add a little hot water to the apricot jam, boil it and then sieve it, so the jam loses its tang. If you want a thicker glaze, add a bit of lemon juice (for the pectin).

Like good dairy products and olive oil, fruit forms an important part of my baking because I feel strongly that all food, even cakes, should be as nutritional as possible. I value how fruit fortifies your body as well as your mind. I also love how fruit nurtures all the senses – how citrus picks you up in the winter months, while oranges remind me of my time spent in Morocco and berries epitomise childhood summers.

Fruit and Berries

# One-Bowl Yogurt Cake Base Mix

You can add pretty much any fruit you like to this base mix, but the offshoots I give here are favourites at the bakehouse. Once you get the hang of this recipe, I hope you'll go on to use up any surplus seasonal fruit. This mixture can be cooked either in a loaf tin or a round cake tin for a birthday celebration or baked in a 12-hole muffin tin, in which case reduce to the cooking time to 25 minutes.

**Makes 1 loaf cake**

• 900-g/2-lb loaf tin, lined with baking parchment and then greased well with oil

150g soft light brown sugar
250g live natural yogurt
50ml pomace oil (or light virgin olive oil)
200g organic plain white flour
75g ground almonds
1 teaspoon baking powder
½ teaspoon bicarbonate of soda
½ teaspoon fine sea salt

Preheat the oven to 200°C/Fan 180°C/Gas 6.

In a large bowl, combine the sugar, yogurt and oil, then add the flour, ground almonds, baking powder, bicarbonate of soda and salt. Continue to mix until combined. At this point, add any fruit to the batter following the instructions on the following pages 48–9.

Pour the cake batter into the lined, greased loaf tin. Bake in the centre of the hot oven for 1 hour or until it springs back to the touch. Leave the cake in the tin to cool.

When stored in an airtight container in the fridge, this basic loaf cake will keep for 7 days. The offshoots that follow over pages 48–9 will keep for 5 days due to their fruit content.

TO FERMENT THE BASE MIX
Once mixed, store the cake batter in an airtight container in the fridge for 3 days to allow it to ferment. This helps to develop the flavours and allows the fruit to ferment a little.

To ferment: Once mixed, store the cake batter in an airtight container in the fridge for 3 days to allow the mixture to ferment.

## Apple or Pear Yogurt Cake

*Many varieties of eating apples are now grown for their sweetness, so I encourage you to seek out cooking apples for this cake for their lovely tart flavour. The pear cake is simply a variation of the apple one, which we make at Fortitude whenever we have a glut of pears to use up.*

250g cooking apples, peeled and cut into
  2.5-cm/1-inch cubes
4 tablespoons maple syrup
½ teaspoon ground cinnamon
*or*
2 medium pears
Juice of 1 lemon

For the apple cake, cook the diced apple with the maple syrup and ground cinnamon in a pan over medium heat for 15 minutes or until almost cooked down. Leave to cool completely. For the pear cake, grate the pears into a bowl, add the lemon juice and leave to soak for 10 minutes.

Fold the fruit into the base cake mixture. Either leave the cake batter to ferment (see above) or bake it straightaway.

When ready, bake the cake following the instructions on page 46.

When stored in an airtight container in the fridge, this cake will keep for 5 days.

## Blood Orange Yogurt Cake

*These ruby-coloured blood oranges are in season in the UK only from Christmas time to the end of February, so there is just a short window of opportunity to make the most of them.*

Zest and juice of 2 organic, unwaxed
  blood oranges
1 tablespoon orange flower water
2 tablespoons Seville orange marmalade
  (see page 181)
1 blood orange, peeled and segmented,
  to decorate
Ground cinnamon, to dust

Combine the zest and juice of the 2 blood oranges with the orange flower water and Seville orange marmalade. Fold the orange mixture into the base cake mixture. Either leave the cake batter to ferment (see above) or bake it straightaway.

When ready, bake the cake following the instructions on page 46. Leave the cake to cool slightly. Before serving, decorate with blood orange segments and dust with a sprinkling of ground cinnamon.

When stored in an airtight container in the fridge, this cake will keep for 5 days.

## Damson and Sage Yogurt Cake

*I love damsons. My father often came home with a pocketful. Once ripened on the kitchen windowsill, we ate them cooked down with a few tablespoons of sugar and served alongside double-cream rice pudding. I make this damson and sage cake each summer; it is always the first one to be demolished.*

12 damsons, stoned and each cut into
  8 pieces
2 tablespoons unrefined golden caster
  sugar
50ml cold water
½ tablespoon finely chopped sage

Cook the chopped damsons with the sugar and water in a pan over a medium heat for 10 minutes or until softened. Leave to cool completely. Fold the chopped sage and three-quarters of the cooled damsons into the base cake mixture. (Reserve the rest of the damsons for decorating the top of the cake.) Either leave the cake batter to ferment (see above) or bake it straightaway.

When ready, bake the cake following the instructions on page 46. Leave the cake to cool slightly. Before serving, decorate by pouring over the reserved damsons.

When stored in an airtight container in the fridge, this cake will keep for 5 days.

## Apricot Yogurt Cake

*Each year at Fortitude, we use apricots while they are in season throughout June and July. We also preserve the fruits in syrup so that, on the days when the sun is no longer shining, we can use preserved apricots in exactly same way as fresh.*

9 fresh or preserved fizzy apricots
  (see page 183)
Zest and juice of 1 organic, unwaxed lemon
1 teaspoon vanilla extract
1 tablespoon flaked almonds, to decorate
Apricot jam, warmed, to glaze

Stone 6 of the apricots and cut them into 8 pieces each. Fold the chopped apricots, lemon zest and juice and vanilla extract into the base cake mixture. Either leave the cake batter to ferment (see above) or bake it straightaway.

When ready to bake, stone the remaining 3 apricots and cut them into 6 pieces each. Bake the cake following the instructions on page 46, but scatter the apricot pieces over the top. Leave the cake to cool slightly. Before serving, decorate by sprinkling the flaked almonds over the centre of the cake. Brush the top of the cake with warmed apricot jam.

When stored in an airtight container in the fridge, this cake will keep for 5 days.

*From left to right:*
Damson and Sage Yogurt
Cake, Apricot Yogurt Cake.

Fruit and Berries

# White Grape *and* Rosemary Cake

This cake was the result of my greengrocer delivering bunches of grapes every week, even though I hadn't ordered them. Because our fruit and veg deliveries are seasonal, they are often made up of whatever our supplier has a glut of. Reducing wastage is not without its challenges – it keeps us on our toes – but can result in a happy accident, like this grape and rosemary pairing.

**Makes 1 loaf cake or 8 small cakes**

- 900-g/2-lb loaf tin, lined with baking parchment and then greased well with butter or a well-greased 8-hole muffin tin

250g organic self-raising white flour
¼ teaspoon bicarbonate of soda
65g ground almonds
Pinch of fine sea salt
6 small eggs
350g unrefined golden caster sugar
150g salted butter, very soft – almost liquid
180g live natural yogurt
150g white grapes, squashed
2 teaspoons finely chopped rosemary
1 tablespoon icing sugar

**To decorate**
Small bunch of white grapes
1 egg white, beaten
Caster sugar

Preheat the oven to 200°C/Fan 180°C/Gas 6.

Sift together the flour and bicarbonate of soda in a bowl, then add the ground almonds and salt.

Place the eggs and golden caster sugar in the bowl of a mixer and whisk on medium/high for 5 minutes or until light and creamy. Reduce the speed of the mixer and add the flour and almond mixture in three batches, mixing between each addition.

Add the butter to the bowl and mix for 1 minute, then add the yogurt and mix for a further 2 minutes.

Remove the bowl from the stand of the mixer and gently fold the grapes and chopped rosemary through the cake batter by hand until evenly distributed.

Pour the cake batter into the lined loaf tin or divide it equally between the holes of the muffin tin. Smooth the surface and then sift the icing sugar over the top.

Bake for 45 minutes for the loaf cake or 25 minutes for the muffins or until it springs back to the touch and a skewer inserted into the centre comes out clean – this cake can be a bit of a joker, so do check that it's done. Once baked, leave to cool in the tin for at least 1 hour.

Meanwhile, make the crystallised grapes. Dip the bunch of grapes into the beaten egg white and then into a small bowl of caster sugar. Leave the sugary grapes to dry in the turned-off oven once the cake has been removed.

When stored in an airtight container in the fridge, this cake will keep only for a few days because the grapes ferment.

# Blackberry *and* Hazelnut Loaf Cake

During late summer, whenever we have a glut of blackberries, we add them to cakes, custards and jams at the bakehouse. All too soon, the season is over and they are gone for another year. Using toasted hazelnuts, this base is an alternative to our cake with ground almonds.

**Makes 1 loaf cake or 8 small cakes**

- 900-g/2-lb loaf tin, lined with baking parchment and then greased well with butter or a well-greased 8-hole muffin tin

90g hazelnuts
250g organic self-raising white flour
¼ teaspoon bicarbonate of soda
Pinch of fine sea salt
6 small eggs
350g unrefined golden caster sugar
150g salted butter, very soft – almost liquid
180g live natural yogurt
150g blackberries

Preheat the oven to 200°C/Fan 180°C/Gas 6.

Scatter the hazelnuts over a baking tray and place in the oven for 5 minutes or until lightly toasted. When cool enough to handle, wrap the nuts in a clean tea towel and rub vigorously to remove their skins. Place 65g of the nuts in a food processor and blitz to a powder.

Sift together the flour and bicarbonate of soda in a bowl, then add the ground hazelnuts and salt.

Place the eggs and sugar in the bowl of a mixer and whisk on medium/high for 5 minutes or until light and creamy. Reduce the speed and add the flour in three batches, mixing between each addition.

Add the butter to the bowl and mix for 1 minute, then add the yogurt and mix for a further 2 minutes.

Remove the bowl from the stand of the mixer and gently fold the blackberries through the cake batter by hand so they are evenly distributed.

Pour the cake batter into the lined loaf tin or divide it between the holes of the muffin tin. Smooth the surface and scatter the remaining hazelnuts over the top.

Bake for 45 minutes for the loaf cake or 25 minutes for the muffins or until it springs back to the touch. Once baked, leave the cake to cool in the tin for at least 1 hour.

When stored in an airtight container in the fridge, this cake will keep only for a few days.

Fruit and Berries

# Chocolate *and* Prune Cake

I love prunes, but find that they are very under-used in baking. Prunes add a richness and moistness to any cake or tart that you put them in. They are also delicious in porridge with maple syrup and buttermilk. Serve slices of this cake with crème fraîche and a handful of organic blackberries on the side.

**Makes 1 round cake**

- 23-cm/9-inch round springform tin, lined with baking parchment

175g salted butter, softened
365g dark chocolate, broken into pieces
7 eggs, separated
100g unrefined golden caster sugar

**For the prune paste**
185g pitted prunes, finely chopped
65ml warm water
1 teaspoon pomegranate molasses
1 teaspoon dark brown sugar
1 teaspoon good-quality cocoa powder
½ teaspoon fine sea salt

To make the prune paste, place all the ingredients in a pan and simmer over a low heat for 5 minutes, stirring occasionally. Transfer to a food processor and blitz for 1 minute or until smooth. Set aside to cool.

Place the butter and chocolate in a heatproof bowl set over a pan of simmering (but not boiling) water. Stir until melted. Set aside to cool for 10 minutes.

Preheat the oven to 185°C/Fan 165°C/Gas 4.

Once cool, add the prune paste to the chocolate mixture and gently stir to combine. Add the egg yolks one at a time, stirring to combine between each addition.

Place the egg whites into the grease-free bowl of a mixer. Whisk the egg whites while gradually adding the sugar until stiff and glossy. Using a metal spoon, fold the stiff egg whites into the chocolate mixture in three batches. Do not overwork the mixture as you want to keep as much air in as possible.

Pour the cake batter into the lined tin. Bake in the centre of the hot oven for 40 minutes. The cake should still have a good wobble when cooked – do not overbake.

Once baked, leave the cake to cool in the tin for 30 minutes. Remove the cake from the tin and chill in the fridge until ready to serve.

When stored in an airtight container in the fridge, this cake will keep for a few days.

# Bara Brith *with* Honey *and* Cardamom

I first made this recipe many moons ago at Bumblebee as a vegan alternative to Christmas cake. Over the years, I have added honey to the cake mixture but if you do want to keep it vegan, use agave syrup instead. The dried fruit needs to soak overnight in tea before baking.

**Makes 1 loaf cake or 1 round cake**

- 900-g/2-lb loaf tin or 20-cm/8-inch round cake tin, lined with baking parchment

355g organic self-raising wholemeal flour
2 teaspoons ground cardamom
1 teaspoon ground cinnamon
Zest and juice of 1 organic, unwaxed orange
65g raw honey (or agave syrup), plus extra to serve
Salted butter, to serve

**For the fruit mix**
500ml strong tea
200g raisins
200g sultanas
100g currants
50g dried sour cherries
50g prunes, stoned and finely chopped
100g mixed peel

Brew the strong tea. Place the dried fruit and mixed peel in a bowl and pour over the tea. Cover and leave at room temperature to soak overnight.

The next day, when you are ready to bake, preheat the oven to 180°C/Fan 160°C/Gas 4.

Place the flour in a bowl, then add the spices. Gently fold the flour into the tea-soaked fruit, then add the orange zest and juice and honey.

Pour the cake batter into the lined tin and smooth the surface. Bake in the centre of the hot oven for 2 hours, but after the first hour place a snug-fitting strip or disc of baking parchment on top of the cake to stop it from colouring too much. When cooked, the cake will spring back to the touch and a skewer inserted into the centre will come out clean.

Before serving, brush or drizzle the cake with a little warmed honey. Cut into thick slices, spread with a generous amount of butter and drizzle with extra honey.

When stored in an airtight container in the fridge, this cake will keep for 10 days.

# Chocolate *and* Blackberry Loaf Cake

I have been making this cake now for over 20 years. I devised the recipe when Whole Foods ordered a vegan range from my first bakery, Patisserie Organic. This cake does not contain any eggs, of course, and so it is the reaction of the vinegar with the bicarbonate of soda that gives volume. For the first time, I am sharing my original recipe.

**Makes 1 loaf cake or 1 round cake**

- 900-g/2-lb loaf tin or 20-cm/8-inch round tin, lined with baking parchment and greased with pomace oil

200g organic self-raising white flour
½ teaspoon bicarbonate of soda
225g soft light brown sugar
40g good-quality cocoa powder
½ teaspoon fine sea salt
100ml pomace oil (or light virgin olive oil)
1 tablespoon white wine vinegar
220ml oat milk
1 tablespoon pomegranate molasses
1 tablespoon rosewater
150g blackberries, halved, plus extra to serve
Shelled, skinned pistachios, finely chopped (optional)

**For the topping**
200g dark chocolate
2 tablespoons golden syrup

Preheat the oven to 200°C/Fan 180°C/Gas 6.

Sift together the flour and bicarbonate of soda in a bowl, then add the sugar, cocoa powder and salt. Add all the other ingredients, except the blackberries and pistachios, and mix with a wooden spoon until smooth. Gently fold in the blackberries.

Pour the cake batter into the lined tin. Bake in the centre of the hot oven for 45 minutes or until it springs back to the touch.

Once baked, leave the cake to cool in the tin.

Meanwhile, make the topping. Place the chocolate and golden syrup in a heatproof bowl, set the bowl over a pan of simmering (but not boiling) water and stir until melted and fully combined.

When cool, remove the cake from the tin and spread over the chocolate topping. If you like, decorate with chopped pistachios, and serve with extra blackberries.

When stored in an airtight container in the fridge, this cake will keep for 5 days.

# Orange *and* Almond Little Buns

We make this recipe every day at the bakehouse in the form of a loaf cake – it is possibly our most popular at Fortitude – but for a change, I have baked them as little buns in a mould or muffin tin.

**Makes 8 little buns**

- 6-hole silicone bun mould or muffin tin (use two moulds or bake in two batches)

2 large oranges
250g ground almonds
2 teaspoons baking powder
6 eggs
250g unrefined golden
   caster sugar

**For the syrup**
100g unrefined golden
   caster sugar
Juice and zest of 1 large
   organic, unwaxed orange
100ml water
1 tablespoon orange flower
   water

**For the topping**
Apricot jam, warmed, to glaze
2 tablespoons shelled skinned
   pistachios, finely chopped

Place the oranges in a pan with a tight-fitting lid and add enough water to cover the fruit. Place the lid on the pan and bring the water to the boil over a high heat. Reduce the heat and simmer until the oranges are completely soft – this takes about 1 hour. Remove the oranges from the water using a slotted spoon and leave to cool completely. Once cool, transfer the whole oranges to a food processor and purée until smooth.

Preheat the oven to 200°C/Fan 180°C/Gas 6.

Combine the ground almonds and baking powder in a bowl.

Place the eggs and sugar in the bowl of a mixer and whisk on medium/high for 5 minutes or until light, creamy and trebled in volume. Reduce the speed to low and add the almond mixture in three batches along with the orange purée, mixing between each addition.

Leave the cake batter to sit for 10 minutes, then place the bun mould or muffin tin on a baking tray and divide the batter equally between the holes. Bake for 25 minutes or until firm to the touch. Once baked, leave the buns to cool in the mould or tin.

To make the syrup, combine all the ingredients in a pan and bring to the boil over a high heat. Reduce the heat to low and simmer the syrup for a few minutes until it starts to thicken.

Pour the warm syrup into a shallow dish. When the buns are cool, remove them from the moulds and rest them top-side down in the syrup. Leave to soak for 3 minutes.

Before serving, glaze the tops of the buns with the warmed jam, sprinkle with chopped pistachios and spoon over a little extra syrup.

When stored in an airtight container in the fridge, these buns will keep for 5–7 days.

# Lemon *and* Olive Oil Little Buns

We were one of the first to make olive oil polenta cakes in London, at Patisserie Organic, and I soon turned to making buns when we found silicone bun moulds. These are lovely served with vanilla ice cream and baked peaches.

**Makes 8 little buns**

- 6-hole silicone bun mould or muffin tin (use two moulds or bake in two batches)

210ml pomace oil (or light virgin olive oil)
4 eggs
145g unrefined golden caster sugar
Zest of 2 large organic, unwaxed lemons (reserve the juice for the syrup)
145g fine polenta flour
100g ground almonds
1½ teaspoons baking powder

**For the syrup**
100g unrefined golden caster sugar
Juice of 2 large lemons (see above)
100ml water

Preheat the oven to 200°C/Fan 180°C/Gas 6.

To make the buns, combine all the ingredients in a bowl and whisk vigorously using a hand whisk for 4 minutes until it forms a thick batter.

Place the bun mould or muffin tin on a baking tray. Divide the cake batter equally between the bun holes, filling each hole almost to the top. Bake in the centre of the hot oven for 25 minutes or until the buns are brown and slightly domed on top. Once baked, leave the buns in the mould or tin until completely cool.

To make the syrup, combine all the ingredients in a pan and bring to the boil over a high heat. Reduce the heat to low and simmer the syrup for a few minutes until it starts to thicken.

Pour the warm syrup into a flat, shallow dish. When the buns are cool, remove them from the moulds and rest them top-side down in the syrup. Leave to soak for 3 minutes.

When stored in an airtight container in the fridge, these buns will keep for 7 days.

# Candied Fig Devonshire Little Buns

When I first made cream buns, I had just been given two jars of Greek spoon sweets (sweet preserves served on a spoon) by Monica at Odysea Foods, so I added candied fig to the filling. I use milk instead of egg wash here as traditional Devonshire splits are not shiny. You can use dried yeast, but I prefer fresh for its slower reaction – the buns don't rise as fast, which results in a better texture. You don't need to buy a whole block as Planet Organic sell small cubes of biodynamic yeast.

**Makes 6 little buns**

• 1 large baking tray, lined with baking parchment

150ml full-fat milk, plus extra to brush

5g fresh yeast (or 3g dried yeast)

1 teaspoon sugar

250g organic plain white flour

50g unrefined golden caster sugar

¼ teaspoon fine sea salt

55g unsalted butter, melted

**To finish**

300ml double cream

3 candied fig pieces, cut in half or very finely chopped

2 teaspoons icing sugar

6 teaspoons fig jam (see page 183)

Heat the milk in a pan over a low heat until lukewarm. Crumble the yeast into the milk, then add the sugar and give it a quick stir. Cover and leave for 10 minutes.

Place the flour, caster sugar, salt and butter in the bowl of a mixer and add the milk. Using the dough hook, mix for 6 minutes or until well combined and elastic. Cover the bowl with food wrap and leave for 1 hour in a warm place. When the dough pushes back against the palm of your hand, it is ready to roll.

Preheat the oven to 220°C/Fan 200°C/Gas 7.

Divide the dough into 6 equal pieces and roll each into a ball: with the palm of your hand cupped over the dough, move it around on a floured surface for 15 seconds. Place the balls on a lined baking tray. Leave for 5 minutes and then brush the tops with milk. Bake for 15 minutes or until brown. Once baked, leave to cool completely.

Using an electric whisk, whip the cream until thick and fold in 1 teaspoon of the icing sugar. If using finely chopped figs, fold them into the whipped cream.

Split the buns across the middle at a slight angle, but don't cut through to the other side. Spread the fig jam onto the bottom half of each bun and pipe or spread the whipped cream on top. If using halved figs, place one inside each bun. Dust the buns with the remaining icing sugar. Eat straightaway.

# Raspberry *and* Coconut Little Buns

This is one of our most popular gluten-free desserts, which also came about almost by accident when 50kg of desiccated coconut was delivered to us by mistake (twice our normal order). Now we make hundreds of these buns each week that we sell at the bakehouse and deliver to our wholesale customers, who order them in large quantities because they keep really well.

**Makes 8 little buns**

- 6-hole silicone bun mould or muffin tin (use two moulds or bake in two batches)

250g ground almonds
90g desiccated coconut
1 teaspoon baking powder
200g salted butter, softened
250g unrefined golden caster sugar
6 small eggs
1 teaspoon vanilla extract
125g fresh raspberries, plus extra to serve
1 tablespoon icing sugar, to dust

Combine the ground almonds, desiccated coconut and baking powder in a bowl.

Place the butter and sugar in the bowl of a mixer and beat with a paddle attachment on high speed for 6 minutes. Add the eggs in three batches, mixing between each addition. Next, add the vanilla extract.

Reduce the speed of the mixer to slow and add the almond and coconut mixture in three batches. Finally fold in the raspberries by hand. Once combined, put the mixing bowl in the fridge for 35 minutes.

Preheat the oven to 200°C/Fan 180°C/Gas 6.

Place the bun mould or muffin tin on a baking tray and divide the batter equally between the holes. Bake in the centre of the hot oven for 25 minutes or until firm to the touch. Once baked, leave the buns in the mould or tin until completely cool.

Before serving, dust with icing sugar and top with a few raspberries.

When stored in an airtight container in the fridge, these buns will keep for 7 days. You can put them back into a hot oven (200°C/Fan 180°C/Gas 6) for 6 minutes and they will crisp up but still stay moist in the middle.

# Blueberry *and* Lime Little Buns

We make these often at the bakery for our vegan customers. You can add any seasonal fruit to the base mix, which can last, covered, in the fridge for up to a week – it just needs a quick stir before use.

**Makes 12 little buns**

- 6-hole silicone bun mould or muffin tin (use two moulds or bake in two batches)

350g organic plain white flour
2 teaspoons baking powder
125g unrefined golden caster sugar
¼ teaspoon bicarbonate of soda
¼ teaspoon fine sea salt
250ml oat milk
1 teaspoon cider vinegar
60ml pomace oil (or light virgin olive oil)
Zest and juice of 2 organic, unwaxed limes
150g fresh blueberries

Place all the ingredients together in a bowl, except the blueberries. Whisk vigorously with a hand whisk until smooth. Leave to rest for 30 minutes.

Preheat the oven to 200°C/Fan 180°C/Gas 6.

Gently fold the blueberries into the mix by hand.

Place the bun mould or muffin tray on a baking tray. Divide the cake batter equally between the holes of the 2 bun moulds and bake immediately. Alternatively, bake one batch of 6 buns and keep the rest of the batter to bake a second batch over the next 7 days.

Bake in the centre of the hot oven for 25 minutes or until a skewer inserted into the centre comes out clean – this is another deceptive bake, as many vegan bakes are, so check first. Leave the buns in the tray to cool.

When stored in an airtight container, these buns will keep for a few days.

TO FERMENT
Once mixed, store the cake batter in an airtight container in the fridge for up to 7 days. Before baking, stir the mixture briefly to reincorporate the oil.

# Dairy

A lot of people tell me that my baking at Fortitude has a distinctive style. They describe that style in many different ways – slightly rustic, yet elegant, not like a cake, not too sweet – but what all the people always say is that my bakes taste of home and of childhood. In many ways, they are old-fashioned in style (if not in method): natural and wholesome, soft and tangy, not overly sweet, even a little bit farmyard-y. Basically, I'm trying to recreate the tastes that I enjoyed during my childhood in Ireland. That is my inspiration.

I believe food should be good for you and even cakes can offer nutrition by using natural ingredients rather than synthetic pastes or excessive amounts of sugar. This isn't about being holier than thou: I simply prefer to use starters and ferments to amplify the flavours of seasonal ingredients. I realised this through watching how my mother and grandmother used whatever ingredients they had around them and understanding how they got the very best from them. My initial idea for a book was 'Food from the Fields': recipes showcasing those flavours of the farm and the fields, using ingredients that tasted of where they came from, which I couldn't find when I arrived in London.

My travels through Morocco are another influence on my baking. In the countryside where my mother-in-law lives, they fortify butter with salt and then leave it until it is close to going off. You can imagine the smell – like a full-on, powerful cheese. My mother-in-law and her family are really good cooks and make their own couscous. They add this fortified butter (known as smem) to the couscous or to broths to create an amazing depth of flavour. The Lemon, Poppy Seed and Goat's Milk Cake (see page 76) and Orange, Yogurt and Polenta Cake (see page 78) are the only batters in this chapter that you can leave to ferment, but many others use live yogurt or fermented butter to add the same intensity of flavour that my mother's and grandmother's bakes had, especially in the simple butter biscuits. My recipe for fermented butter can be found in Storecupboard chapter (see page 178), though you can also use a good-quality salted butter.

On that note, I want to say that salt plays a huge part in my cooking. I prefer to use Maldon sea salt or fleur de sel de Guérande. And I always use salted butter when baking, rather than adding salt, which I think makes for a different and better result.

# Walnut Butter Loaf Cake
## *with* Labneh *and* Honey

Eaten with homemade labneh and raw honey warmed through with a teaspoon of orange flower water, this cake is more of a dessert than a tea-time cake. Because walnuts are oily, I find they have a tendency to split the mixture unless they are added after the flour. For the same reason, this loaf does not keep for quite as long as other cakes once baked.

**Makes 1 loaf cake**

Preheat the oven to 220°C/Fan 200°C/Gas 7.

• 900-g/2-lb loaf tin, lined
  with baking parchment

Place the butter and sugar in the bowl of a mixer and beat with a paddle attachment on medium speed for 5 minutes. Add the eggs one at a time, mixing between each addition.

225g salted butter, very soft
225g unrefined golden
  caster sugar
3 eggs
225g organic self-raising
  white flour
225g shelled walnuts, finely
  chopped
50g live natural yogurt
1 tablespoon pomegranate
  molasses

Reduce the speed of the mixer to slow and add the flour in three batches, making sure it is well combined. Finally, fold in the walnuts, yogurt and pomegranate molasses by hand.

Pour the cake batter into the lined loaf tin and bake for 40 minutes or until it springs back to the touch. Leave the cake in the tin to cool.

**To serve**
2 tablespoons raw honey
1 teaspoon orange
  flower water
Homemade labneh
  (see page 180)

Before serving, gently warm the honey and stir through the orange flower water. Serve thick slices of the cake, each with a generous spoonful of labneh and drizzled with a teaspoon of warm honey.

When stored in an airtight container in the fridge, this loaf cake will keep for 3 days.

# Lemon, Poppy Seed *and* Goat's Milk Loaf Cake

Slightly tangy and not overly sweet, this cake is really lovely served with Assam tea. During my time at Bumblebee, I baked with many different kinds of milks, including a goat's milk cake for those who had trouble digesting cow's milk. This cake also uses goat's milk and is one of the first cakes I made when I opened Fortitude.

**Makes 1 loaf cake**

- 900-g/2-lb loaf tin, lined with baking parchment

180g salted butter, very soft
180g unrefined golden caster sugar
4 small eggs
235g organic self-raising white flour
180ml goat's milk
Zest and juice of 2 organic, unwaxed lemons
75g poppy seeds (see 'to ferment' note)
Pinch of fine sea salt

Preheat the oven to 200°C/Fan 180°C/Gas 6.

Place all the ingredients in the bowl of a mixer and beat with the paddle attachment on medium speed for 6 minutes.

Pour the cake batter into the lined loaf tin and bake for 75 minutes or until completely set and it springs back to the touch. Leave the cake in the tin to cool.

When stored in an airtight container in the fridge, this loaf cake will keep for 5 days.

TO FERMENT
Once mixed, store the cake batter for up to 5 days in an airtight container in the fridge to allow the mixture to ferment. You can also soak the poppy seeds overnight in the goat's milk.

# Sticky Porter Cake
*with* Buttermilk

This is a cake my mother has always made. There is no better baker of fruit cakes in the world than my mother; watching her soaking fruit, zesting citrus and feeding a cake with whiskey over the weeks before Christmas ignited my passion for baking. I can't smell mixed spice without thinking of her old cake tins, wrapped in thick brown paper and tied with string, to stop the cakes catching. The raisins and sultanas need to soak overnight in the buttermilk before using.

**Makes 1 round cake**

- 20-cm/8-inch round cake tin with deep sides (at least 18cm/7 inches), lined with baking parchment and greased well with butter

200g raisins
200g sultanas
250ml buttermilk (see page 180)
400g organic plain white flour
100g organic light rye flour
1 teaspoon ground cinnamon
1 teaspoon ground nutmeg
½ teaspoon ground mace
1½ teaspoons baking powder
½ teaspoon fine sea salt
230g fermented butter (see page 178) or good-quality salted butter, softened
230g dark muscovado sugar
50g dried sour cherries
50g sweet and salty preserved lemons (see page 182), very finely chopped
3 eggs
250ml porter (or stout or other dark beers)

Place the raisins and sultanas in a bowl and pour over the buttermilk. Cover and leave overnight at room temperature.

The next day, preheat the oven to 180°C/Fan 160°C/Gas 4.

Take a piece of baking parchment and double it over, making sure it is at least 25cm/10 inches high. Wrap it around the outside of the lined cake tin and tie in place with string.

In a large bowl, combine the flours, spices, baking powder and salt. Add the butter and crumble through, working it for 5 minutes.

Add the sugar, cherries and lemons to the bowl, then fold through with the soaked dried fruit and buttermilk.

In a separate bowl, whisk together the eggs and porter. Add this mixture to the cake batter and beat vigorously with a wooden spoon.

Pour the cake batter into the lined tin, smooth the surface and bake for 3 hours. When cooked, the cake will spring back to the touch and a skewer inserted into the centre will come out clean. Leave the cake in the tin to cool.

When wrapped in baking parchment and stored in a cool, dry place or in the fridge, this cake will keep for up to 2 weeks.

Dairy

# Orange, Yogurt
## *and* Polenta Cake

In the same way that live natural yogurt gives such a soft crumb to my soda bread, it also plumps up the polenta mixture used to make this orange cake: the dairy softens the bite of the polenta, resulting in a texture more like the Middle-Eastern semolina cake, basbousa, or an old-fashioned semolina pudding. The yogurt also gives the cake a tangy complexity, amplified by the sharpness of the citrus. If you would rather bake individual cakes, this mixture also makes delicious muffins with the addition of a few berries. Bake these for 25 minutes.

**Makes 1 loaf cake**

• 900-g/2-lb loaf tin, lined
  with baking parchment and
  greased well with oil

250g fine polenta flour
45g organic buckwheat flour
½ teaspoon fine sea salt
1½ teaspoons baking powder
130g unrefined golden
  caster sugar
130g salted butter, very soft
Zest and juice of 2 organic,
  unwaxed oranges
4 large eggs
85g live natural yogurt

**For the caramelised oranges**
300ml water
150g caster sugar
2 oranges, sliced

Preheat the oven to 220°C/Fan 200°C/Gas 7.

Place all the ingredients in the bowl of a mixer and beat with a paddle attachment on medium speed for 5 minutes or until well combined.

Spoon the cake batter into the lined loaf tin. Bake for 1 hour or until it springs back to the touch. Leave the cake in the tin to cool.

To make the caramelised oranges, pour the water into a pan and add the sugar and orange slices. Simmer for 15 minutes. Drain and arrange the caramelised orange slices over the top of the cake.

When stored in an airtight container in the fridge, this loaf cake will keep for 7 days.

TO FERMENT
Once mixed, store the cake batter for up to 7 days in an airtight container in the fridge to allow the mixture to ferment. Before baking, mix the batter briefly to reincorporate.

# Fermented Butter
# Breton Biscuits

These simple tea-time biscuits are pleasingly chunky and a little old-fashioned. I first saw Bretons being made in a small French bakery in the new town of Marrakech. They were more spit-and-sawdust than mine – they didn't use as much butter, so they were similar to a rusk – but they inspired me to make these. I prefer fermented butter, but a good-quality salted butter can be used also. The dough will keep well in the fridge for up to 2 weeks, so you can slice 1-cm/½-inch thick rounds from the log whenever you want to bake off a few biscuits.

**Makes 20 biscuits**

• 1 large baking tray, lined
  with baking parchment

230g fermented butter
  (see page 178) or
  good-quality salted butter
230g organic plain white flour
200g demerara sugar

Place the butter, flour and 100g of the sugar in the bowl of a mixer and beat with a paddle attachment on medium speed until everything comes together to form a dough.

Roll the dough into a log about 5cm/2 inches in diameter. Lay a piece of baking parchment on your work surface and sprinkle the remaining sugar over the parchment. Roll the dough log in the sugar to form a thick crust.

Wrap the dough log in the parchment, twisting at both ends to secure. Chill the dough in the fridge for at least 2 hours.

Preheat the oven to 200°C/Fan 180°C/Gas 6.

When ready to bake, take the dough log out of the fridge and slice into 1-cm/½-inch thick rounds. Place the rounds on a lined baking tray. Depending on the fat content of the butter, the biscuits might spread a little, so space the rounds about 5cm/2 inches apart. Bake for 30 minutes or until golden brown – don't worry that they've gone too far because they should be rusk-like. Leave the biscuits on the tray to cool.

Once cool, store in an airtight container at room temperature. The biscuits can be baked again for 8 minutes in a 200°C/Fan 180°C/Gas 6 oven to crisp up.

# Ginger *and* Sea Salt Butter Biscuits

In the run up to Christmas, we bake hundreds of these gingery, buttery biscuits at Fortitude to sell in clear bags tied up with string. You can also turn them into a pudding as they are delicious served alongside vanilla ice cream mixed with chopped stem ginger and a simple chocolate sauce poured over.

**Makes 28 biscuits**

- 3 large baking trays, lined with baking parchment and greased well with butter

275g organic plain white flour
2 teaspoons ground ginger
½ teaspoon ras el hanout (see page 176)
1 teaspoon fine sea salt, plus extra to sprinkle
100g salted butter
25g golden syrup
125g dark muscavado sugar
2 eggs

Preheat the oven to 200°C/Fan 180°C/Gas 6.

In a large bowl, sift together the flour, spices and salt.

Place the butter, golden syrup and sugar in the bowl of a mixer and beat with a paddle attachment on high speed for 5 minutes or until creamed lightly together. Add the eggs, one at a time, mixing between each addition.

Reduce the speed of the mixer to slow and gradually add large tablespoons of the flour mixture to make a dough.

Once completely combined, divide the dough into 28 pieces, each weighing 24g. Wet your hands and roll each piece of dough into a tight, smooth ball.

Place the dough balls on the lined and buttered baking trays. The biscuits might spread a little, so space the balls about 5cm/2 inches apart. Sprinkle with sea salt and bake for 15 minutes or until golden brown. Halfway through the cooking time, turn the sheet around in the oven. Leave the biscuits on the sheets to cool.

Once cool, store in an airtight container at room temperature. The biscuits can be baked again for 8 minutes in a 200°C/Fan 180°C/Gas 6 oven to crisp up.

# Chocolate *and* Rye Biscuits *with* Peanut Buttercream

I love the pairing of rye and chocolate in these biscuits, which are sandwiched together with peanut buttercream to make a whoopie pie. This recipe came out of a collaboration between Fortitude Bakehouse and Pump Street Bakery, whose Ecuadorian chocolate works perfectly in these biscuits.

**Makes 10 biscuits or
5 sandwiched biscuits**

• 1 large baking tray, lined
 with baking parchment

30g salted butter
225g dark chocolate
 (minimum 70% cocoa solids)
 broken into pieces
3 eggs
110g soft dark brown sugar
75g organic rye flour
½ teaspoon bicarbonate
 of soda
½ teaspoon fine sea salt
1 teaspoon good-quality cocoa
 powder, to dust

**For the buttercream**
120g salted butter, softened
2 tablespoons crunchy
 peanut butter
½ teaspoon vanilla extract
2 tablespoons icing sugar

Place the butter and chocolate in a heatproof bowl, set the bowl over a pan of simmering (but not boiling) water and stir gently until melted and fully combined. Set aside to cool for 5 minutes.

Place the eggs and sugar in the bowl of a mixer and beat with a whisk attachment on high speed for 5 minutes or until light and fluffy. Gradually fold in the cooled, melted chocolate.

Combine the rye flour, bicarbonate of soda and salt in a small bowl. Using a large metal spoon, fold the flour into the chocolate mixture. Cover the bowl and chill in the fridge for 2 hours. It's important that the biscuit dough is cold as it will be impossible to handle otherwise.

Preheat the oven to 200°C/Fan 180°C/Gas 6.

When ready to bake, take the dough out of the fridge, quickly divide it into 10 equal pieces, then shape each piece into a round. Lightly press the rounds onto a lined baking tray to gently flatten them into patties. Bake for 25 minutes or until set and slightly cracked on top (like amaretti). Leave the biscuits to cool on the baking tray.

Meanwhile, make the buttercream. Place all the ingredients in the bowl of a mixer and beat with a paddle attachment on high speed for 4 minutes. Transfer to a piping bag with a wide nozzle.

When cool, pipe the buttercream in three stripes across the top of half the biscuits and dust with cocoa powder.

Top each with another biscuit to make a sandwich and dust again with more cocoa powder.

When stored in an airtight container, the biscuits (without the buttercream) will keep for up to 7 days.

*From left to right:* Fermented Butter Breton Biscuits, Ginger and Sea Salt Butter Biscuits, Chocolate and Rye Biscuits with Peanut Buttercream.

# Mont St Michel *with* Cherry Buttercream

I learned the techniques of classic French pâtisserie as part of my three years' training with restaurateur Justin de Blank, during which time we had to make sablé biscuits as part of our daily routine. We made all sorts of shapes and flavours. The Mont St Michel with buttercream is a biscuit that comes from that part of Normandy, in north-west France.

**Makes 8 sandwiched biscuits**

- 2 baking sheets, lined with baking parchment

220g salted butter, softened
130g icing sugar, plus extra
   for dusting
2 large eggs, plus 2 egg yolks
350g organic plain white flour

**For the buttercream**
175g salted butter, softened
80g icing sugar, sifted
12 fresh cherries, stoned
   and finely chopped
½ teaspoon pomegranate
   molasses

**To decorate**
Cherry jam
Fresh cherries

Place the butter and icing sugar in the bowl of a mixer and beat with a paddle attachment on medium speed for 5 minutes. Add the eggs and egg yolks in three batches, mixing between each addition.

Reduce the speed of the mixer to slow and add the flour in three batches. Beat for 3 minutes until everything is completely combined and comes together to form a dough. Remove the dough from the bowl, cover it in food wrap and chill in the fridge for 1 hour.

Preheat the oven to 200°C/Fan 180°C/Gas 6.

When ready to bake, lightly flour your work surface and rolling pin. Roll out the dough to 5mm/¼ inch thick, moving it regularly over the floured surface to prevent it sticking. Using a 7.5-cm/3-inch round cutter, cut out 16 rounds. Place on lined baking sheets and bake for 18 minutes or until golden brown. Leave the biscuits to cool on the baking sheets.

Meanwhile, make the buttercream. Place all the ingredients in the bowl of a mixer and beat with a paddle attachment on high speed for 3 minutes or until creamed.

When cool, spread the buttercream over half the biscuits. Top each with another biscuit to make a sandwich. Pipe or spread a little more buttercream on the top of the sandwiched biscuits and dust with the remaining icing sugar. Spoon over cherry jam and decorate with a couple of whole fresh cherries. Eat straightaway.

# Buckwheat Butter Biscuits

At Moroccan wedding parties, these biscuits are served in big piles as part of the feast. They are made with homemade fermented butter, smem, which gives them an amazing, almost savoury flavour. After the wedding, any leftover biscuits are stored in boxes and then brought out again to enjoy with mint tea or strong coffee. The biscuit dough needs time to chill before baking.

**Makes 48 little biscuits**

• 2 or 3 baking trays, lined with baking parchment

200g organic plain white flour
100g organic buckwheat flour
25g ground almonds
Pinch of fine sea salt
110g fermented butter (see page 178)
135g unrefined golden caster sugar
1 large egg
1 tablespoon rosewater

Combine both the flours into a bowl, then add the ground almonds and salt.

Place the butter and sugar in the bowl of a mixer and beat with a paddle attachment on high speed for 5 minutes.

Reduce the speed of the mixer to slow and add the egg and rosewater. Add the flour mixture, one tablespoon at a time, until everything is completely combined and comes together to form a dough.

Scrape the dough out of the bowl and divide it into two halves. Roll each half into a log about 4cm/1½ inches diameter. Cover the logs in food wrap and chill in the fridge for at least 5 hours or preferably overnight.

Preheat the oven to 210°C/Fan 190°C/Gas 6.

When ready to bake, cut the logs into 5-mm/¼-inch slices. Place on lined baking trays, spacing them about 2.5cm/1 inch apart. Bake for 15 minutes or until golden brown. Halfway through the cooking time, turn the trays around in the oven. Leave the biscuits to cool on the trays.

When stored in an airtight container, these biscuits will keep for up to 7 days.

# Tart Cherry Buns
*with* Sour Cream

These buns were inspired by the Meyers Bageri in Copenhagen. Claus Meyer is a very traditional baker who has never changed his method of baking. His enriched doughs are so simple; he uses them to make buns that can be eaten just with butter. When leaving buns to prove, I find the best way to cover them is to put them in a large food bag and knot it loosely – easy to do and you can reuse the bag. The dough needs to rest overnight and then prove for an hour the next day before baking.

**Makes 9 buns**

- 1 large baking tray, lined with baking parchment and greased well with butter

500g organic plain white flour
2 teaspoons dried yeast (or 28g fresh yeast)
3 tablespoons unrefined golden caster sugar
3 eggs
250g sour cream
115g salted butter, softened
1 teaspoon fine sea salt
125g dried sour cherries
1 egg, beaten, for the egg wash

Place all the ingredients (except the beaten egg for the egg wash) in the bowl of a mixer and mix with a dough hook on medium speed for 7 minutes or until the dough is shiny and a bit springy. Scrape the dough into a container, cover with a lid and leave to rest in the fridge overnight.

When ready to bake the next day, take the dough from the fridge and place on a lightly floured surface. Divide the dough into 9 equal pieces, each weighing about 100g. Roll each piece into a smooth ball: with the palm of your hand cupped over the dough, move it across the floured surface for 15 seconds to shape it into a ball, but don't overwork the dough.

Place the buns on a lined baking tray, cover with a large food bag and tie the end loosely into a knot. Leave to prove in a warm place for 1 hour.

Preheat the oven to 200°C/Fan 180°C/Gas 6.

Remove the food bag from the tray, then brush each bun all over with the egg wash and bake for 25 minutes or until golden brown.

As these are day buns, they won't keep much longer than 24 hours.

# Sticky Cinnamon Buns
## *with* Molasses Sugar

We make these cinnamon buns each day at Fortitude – they are our breakfast offering along with morning brioche buns, and have been on the counter since we opened. The Rapha cyclists love these sticky buns. The dough needs to rest overnight before baking.

**Makes 6 buns**

• 6-hole silicone bun mould
   or muffin tin, greased well
   with butter

500g organic plain white flour
2 teaspoons dried yeast
   (or 28g fresh yeast)
3 tablespoons unrefined
   golden caster sugar
3 eggs
250ml full-fat milk
115g salted butter, softened
1 teaspoon fine sea salt
1 egg, beaten, for the
   egg wash

**For the filling**
225g molasses sugar or
   dark muscovado sugar
2 tablespoons ground
   cinnamon
200g salted butter, softened

One day ahead, make the dough. Place all the ingredients (except the beaten egg for the egg wash) in the bowl of a mixer and mix with a dough hook on medium speed for 7 minutes or until the dough is shiny and a bit springy. Scrape the dough into a container, cover with a lid and leave to rest in the fridge overnight.

When ready to bake the next day, make the filling. Combine all the ingredients in a bowl and beat vigorously with a wooden spoon until well combined.

Take the dough from the fridge and place on a lightly floured surface. Roll the dough out into a 45 x 35-cm/18 x 14-inch rectangle.

Spread the filling evenly over the dough using a palette knife, leaving a 1-cm/½-inch clear margin all the way round.

With the longest edge closest to you, roll up the dough into a log, like a Swiss roll. Keep the roll as tight as possible.

Cut the log into 6 even slices, each about 7.5cm/3 inches thick.

Push each round into a hole of the muffin tin.

Preheat the oven to 200°C/Fan 180°C/Gas 6.

Brush the top of each bun generously with the egg wash. Bake for 25 minutes or until dark golden brown and the sugar is bubbling and caramelised. Halfway through the cooking time, turn the tray around. Transfer the buns to a wire cooling rack to cool.

To freshen up the next day, warm in a 200°C/Fan 180°C/Gas 6 oven for 3 minutes.

# Spices *and* Aromatics

Thinking back to my childhood in Ireland, strong flavours were always a part of the food we ate. Not in savoury dishes, which were very simple and cooked well, but in the cakes my mother baked. It came naturally to my mother to put spices such as cinnamon, nutmeg or cardamom into her bakes, even though that was considered unusual in those days and these kinds of ingredient were far harder to get hold of than they are nowadays. Her fruit cakes paired apples and berries with cinnamon, nutmeg and white pepper – which is much less commonly used now – as well as treacle, golden syrup and crystallised ginger.

I've always understood how spices worked with fruit, but it was while working for restaurateur Justin de Blank that I first made a pain d'épices (see page 104). At Bumblebee I had free access to what they call The Nut Shop; a holistic storecupboard brimming with nuts, dried fruits, honeys and spices. Bumblebee placed emphasis on spices for their health properties; I used to freshly grind mace, cloves, cardamom, fennel and caraway seeds – they all smelled amazing.

On my first trip to Morocco, I was fascinated by how people flavoured their dishes using honey, rosewater and orange flower water, and I learned how Moroccans make their own spice mixes for tagines and use ras el hanout almost how Indians use garam masala, to thicken dishes such as couscous towards the end of their cooking.

Wandering through the spice souk in Marrakech is a feast for the senses. Spices are piled high and the smell is overwhelming. Cumin is always the predominant smell for me and sometimes I roast apple with cumin seeds to serve with savoury dishes like roast pork. The best thing about the spice souk is chatting with the spice sellers; everyone has a story and each stall believes they sell the best blends. The sharing of food and recipes in Morocco is pure joy, although the sharing of a spice blend recipe is a closely guarded family secret and rarely revealed. I chat about baking to them and whenever I mention putting cloves with apples, they can't believe it as clove is a very medicinal spice for Moroccans – they boil the clove in water and drink it for better digestion. I came home to Bumblebee keen to incorporate everything I had learned in Morocco into my own bakes.

My first spice cake was flavoured with ras el hanout and black treacle (see page 98) to create something both slightly sweet yet also savoury – like a Jamaican ginger cake – but really dense, as I had eaten in Morocco. Since then I have used orange flower water and rosewater in biscuits, cakes and syrups to soak sponges with. I add these floral essences to simple butter cake mixes, alongside dried orange peel and cinnamon. In Morocco, you are sprinkled with orange flower water as you drink your cup of tea to keep you fresh and awaken your senses – a holistic way of thinking about spices that really resonated with me.

But the chilli-soaked date and oat loaf cake (see page 103) was inspired by my mother's fruit cakes – she added a honeyed almond paste to the top, like marzipan, but with honey. Oh, the smell was divine. My mother's cakes were renowned in the village and everyone wanted her to make their wedding cakes.

Fruit and spice have a natural affinity. I don't want my fruit to be very sweet but I do want it to have flavour. Rather than adding sugar, especially if the fruit is not at its best, I add cinnamon when roasting peaches, for example. Recently I made a chocolate fondant with Iranian morello cherries and ground cayenne pepper, which accentuated the tartness of the fruit in a good way and gave a warmth to the chocolate, so that it tasted like fruit – that's how I think fruit and spice work well together.

Spices and Aromatics

This recipe came about because I wanted to use dried orange peel in my baking and was looking for flavours that complemented it. Both the orange peel and orange flower water are more fragrant than anything else, so this cake is not so sweet. At the time I wrote this recipe, I was fascinated by kefir – it brings sourness, which I like in cakes. The cinnamon sugar crust is like the traditional crust on a Madeira cake.

**Makes 1 loaf cake**

- 900-g/2-lb loaf tin, lined with baking parchment

Zest and juice of 2 organic, unwaxed oranges

1 teaspoon dried orange peel (available from Organic Herb Trading Co.)

4 tablespoons orange flower water

250g salted butter, softened

250g unrefined golden caster sugar

4 eggs

200g organic self-raising white flour

50g ground almonds

100ml kefir milk or buttermilk (see page 180)

100g demerara sugar

1 teaspoon ground cinnamon

Preheat the oven to 200°C/Fan 180°C/Gas 6.

Place the zest and juice of the fresh oranges in a bowl together with the dried orange peel and orange flower water. Leave for 30 minutes to infuse.

In a large bowl, cream together the butter and sugar using an electric whisk until light and fluffy. Add the eggs one at a time, along with a teaspoon of the flour to prevent curdling, and continue to mix, but do not overmix.

In a separate bowl, combine the flour and ground almonds. Fold this mixture into the creamed butter by hand. Next, fold in the orange mixture and finally the kefir.

Pour the cake batter into the lined loaf tin and smooth the top. Combine the demerara sugar and ground cinnamon, then sprinkle over the top of the cake. Bake for 40 minutes or until it springs back to the touch. Leave the cake to cool in the tin.

When stored in an airtight container in the fridge, this loaf cake will keep for up to 7 days.

# Ras el Hanout *and*
# Black Treacle Loaf Cake

I love this cake decorated with a simple icing and scattered with chilli flakes, which accentuate the warm notes of the ras el hanout used inside the cake. Otherwise, I often glaze this cake while it's still warm with a little bit of apricot jam. It is also delicious eaten warm with a knob of salted butter and a drop of wild honey.

**Makes 1 loaf cake**

• 900-g/2-lb loaf tin, lined with baking parchment

250g organic plain white flour
1 teaspoon bicarbonate of soda
1 tablespoon ras el hanout (see page 176)
¼ teaspoon fine sea salt
250g dark muscovado sugar
2 eggs
180g black treacle or molasses
250ml buttermilk (see page 180)

**For the icing**
150g icing sugar
¼ teaspoon chilli flakes

Preheat the oven to 200°C/Fan 180°C/Gas 6.

Sift together the flour, bicarbonate of soda, ras el hanout and salt in a bowl. Stir in the muscovado sugar.

In a separate bowl, beat together the eggs, treacle and buttermilk. Pour this mixture into the flour and beat vigorously with a wooden spoon until well combined.

Pour the cake batter into the lined loaf tin and bake for 45 minutes or until it springs back to the touch. Leave the cake in the tin to cool.

To make the icing, put the icing sugar in a bowl and add a few drops of warm water until it reaches a runny consistency. Drizzle the icing over the top of the cake, allowing it to run down the sides. Before the icing sets, scatter over the chilli flakes.

When stored in an airtight container in the fridge, this loaf cake will keep for 7 days.

# Roast Apple, Sultana, Pecan *and* Fennel Seed Loaf Cake

Originally, I made this cake at Bumblebee using fennel seeds from the shelves of spices. At that time, I used grated apple, but now I roast the apples and add them to the batter with sultanas and pecans. I love roasting fruit and have always done it. This batter is a lumpy-bumpy mixture with an exquisite aroma and dense texture when baked; it's a far cry from the seed cake I used to make for my father, who only ever wanted plain cakes.

**Makes 1 loaf cake**

- 900-g/2-lb loaf tin, lined with baking parchment

2 cooking apples, unpeeled, cored and chopped into 2.5-cm/1-inch chunks

290g salted butter, softened

1 tablespoon demerara sugar

200g molasses sugar

4 eggs

250g organic self-raising white flour

50g sultanas

50g pecans, finely chopped like breadcrumbs

1 teaspoon fennel seeds

100ml full-fat milk

Preheat the oven to 220°C/Fan 200°C/Gas 7.

Place the apple pieces in a baking dish, then dot with 115g of the butter and sprinkle over the demerara sugar. Roast for 12–15 minutes or until the apples give a little but still keep their shape.

Reduce the oven to 200°C/Fan 180°C/Gas 6.

In a large bowl, cream together the remaining butter and molasses sugar using an electric whisk for 4 minutes or until light and fluffy. Add the eggs one at a time with a teaspoon of the flour to prevent curdling, mixing between each addition.

Fold the remaining flour into the creamed butter using a metal spoon. Fold in the sultanas, pecans, fennel seeds and cooled roast apples by hand. Finally, add the milk and mix until just combined.

Pour the cake batter into the lined loaf tin and bake for 45 minutes or until it springs back to the touch. Leave the cake in the tin to cool.

When stored in an airtight container in the fridge, this loaf cake will keep for 7 days.

# Roast Plum *and* Nutmeg Loaf Cake

This is a really old recipe that I used to make because my father, who worked with dairies, would bring back Mirabelle plums or damsons from the farms that he visited. He would put them on a windowsill to ripen, along with cooking apples and tomatoes. This cake is great with clotted cream or simply by itself.

**Makes 1 loaf cake**

- 900-g/2-lb loaf tin, lined with baking parchment

150g plums, Mirabelles or damsons, stoned and chopped into 1-cm/½-inch pieces
1 tablespoon olive oil
1 tablespoon raw wildflower honey
250g salted butter
250g unrefined golden caster sugar
4 eggs
200g organic self-raising white flour (or 250g Doves Farm gluten-free flour, which is wonderful)
50g ground almonds
2 teaspoons ground nutmeg
100ml full-fat milk
Seedless raspberry jam, warmed, to glaze

Preheat the oven to 180°C/Fan 160°C/Gas 4.

Spread the plum or damson pieces over a roasting tray, toss with the olive oil and drizzle over the honey. Roast for 12–14 minutes or until slightly caramelised.

Increase the oven temperature to 200°C/Fan 180°C/Gas 6.

In a large bowl, cream together the butter and sugar using an electric whisk until light and fluffy. Add the eggs one at a time with a teaspoon of the flour to prevent curdling, mixing between each addition.

In a separate bowl, combine the flour and ground almonds.

Fold the flour and almond mixture into the creamed butter using a metal spoon. Fold in the nutmeg and then finally add the milk.

Pour the cake batter into the lined loaf tin and smooth the top. Gently push the roast plum pieces into the batter along the middle of the loaf. Bake for 45 minutes or until it springs back to the touch. Leave the cake in the tin to cool.

Brush the top of the cake with warmed raspberry jam.

When stored in an airtight container in the fridge, this loaf cake will keep for 7 days.

# Chilli-Soaked Date *and* Oat Loaf Cake

My mother always made sure that we had fruit cake in the house, which we used to eat for breakfast, like those old malt loaves. I'm sure my mother's recipe came from *Woman's Own*, which she got every week. My five sisters and I fought to read that magazine – my sisters loved the gossip columns and problem pages, while I always went straight for the recipes. This cake is inspired by my mother's fruit cake – I've never found better. Before baking, you'll need to soak the dates and oats overnight.

**Makes 1 loaf cake**

- 900-g/2-lb loaf tin, lined with baking parchment

225g dates (preferably Medjool), chopped

95g rolled oats

½ teaspoon chilli powder or ½ teaspoon deseeded and finely chopped fresh red chilli

300ml boiling water

210g salted butter

350g molasses sugar

3 large eggs

250g organic plain wholemeal flour

3 tablespoons black treacle or 4 tablespoons pomegranate molasses

2 teaspoons baking powder

1 teaspoon bicarbonate of soda

1 teaspoon ground cinnamon

½ teaspoon ground nutmeg

½ teaspoon ground cloves

Place the chopped dates, oats and chilli powder in a bowl, then pour over the boiling water. Leave overnight to soak.

The next day, preheat the oven to 200°C/Fan 180°C/Gas 6.

Place the butter and sugar in the bowl of a mixer and beat with a paddle attachment on high speed for 4 minutes or until light but not too fluffy. Add the eggs, one at a time, mixing between each addition.

Combine the flour with all the remaining ingredients in a bowl, then add to the mixer. Give the date and oat mixture a good stir and add that to the mixer too. Mix again until well combined.

Scrape the cake batter into the lined loaf tin and bake for 1 hour 10 minutes or until a skewer comes out clean. Once baked, leave the cake to cool in the tin.

When stored in an airtight container in the fridge, this loaf cake will keep for 7 days.

# Pain d'Épices Loaf Cake

When I first came to London, I worked for restaurateur Justin de Blank. That's where I learned about the French-style pain d'épices. Because he worked organically, Justin had cakes for every time of year and so I learned to use ingredients to match the seasons. At Christmas we made pain d'épices, as well as classic stollen and traditional Christmas cakes. At Fortitude, I make this only in December; I ferment the mix, keeping it for up to a week in the fridge, though you can bake it immediately. Slices of this cake can be eaten toasted and it is also delicious served with cream and poached pears.

**Makes 1 loaf cake**

- 900-g/2-lb loaf tin, lined with baking parchment

350g raw honey
Zest and juice of 1 organic, unwaxed lemon
50g unrefined golden caster sugar
2 tablespoons orange flower water
140g organic plain wholemeal flour
140g organic rye flour
5 teaspoons baking powder
2 tablespoons pain d'épices spice mix (see page 177)
125g sour cream
3 eggs

Preheat the oven to 200°C/Fan 180°C/Gas 6.

Gently warm the honey in a small pan for 5 minutes over a low heat. Take the pan off the heat and add the lemon zest and juice, sugar and orange flower water to the honey.

Combine the flours, baking powder and pain d'épices spice mix in a bowl.

In a large bowl, gently beat together the sour cream and eggs. Stir in the honey mixture and combine. Add the flour and spice mixture – it might seem a little sticky as a result of the rye flour and the copious amounts of honey, but don't worry, it's meant to be sticky.

Scrape the cake batter into the lined loaf tin. Wrap the tin loosely in a cocoon of baking parchment, which will keep the cake soft and give it a lovely rounded shape, rather than splitting on top. Bake for 50 minutes or until it springs back to the touch. Leave the cake in the tin to cool.

When stored in an airtight container at room temperature, this loaf cake will keep for 7–10 days.

TO FERMENT
Once mixed, store the cake batter for up to 7 days in the fridge to allow the mixture to ferment.

# Walnut *and* Stem Ginger Loaf Cake

For my Patisserie Organic bakery, I used to source really tangy yogurt from a farm near Norwich. That was the start of my yogurt obsession. Yogurt gives cake a soft, tangy quality, which goes really well with walnuts, as you'll find in Greece and Morocco. I glaze the top of this cake with the syrup from a jar of stem ginger.

**Makes 1 loaf cake**

- 900-g/2-lb loaf tin, lined with baking parchment

250g salted butter, softened
200g unrefined golden caster sugar
4 eggs
200g organic self-raising white flour
1 teaspoon ground ginger
50g ground walnuts
25g stem ginger from a jar, drained, syrup reserved, and finely chopped, plus extra whole pieces to decorate
50g shelled walnuts, roughly chopped
100g live natural yogurt

Preheat the oven to 200°C/Fan 180°C/Gas 6.

In a large bowl, cream together the butter and sugar using an electric whisk until light and fluffy. Add the eggs one at a time with a teaspoon of the flour to prevent curdling, mixing between each addition.

Fold the remaining flour, ground ginger and ground walnuts into the creamed butter using a metal spoon. Fold in the chopped stem ginger and 30g of the roughly chopped walnuts. Finally, fold in the yogurt.

Pour the cake batter into the lined loaf tin and smooth the top. Sprinkle over the remaining chopped walnuts. Bake for 45 minutes or until it springs back to the touch. Leave the cake in the tin to cool.

To glaze the cake, pour the reserved syrup from the jar of stem ginger over the top of the cake, then scatter over the whole pieces of stem ginger.

When stored in an airtight container in the fridge, this loaf cake will keep for 3–4 days.

# Chocolate *and* Chilli Sugar Olive Oil Loaf Cake

This is another cake from my Patisserie Organic days. We had several Moroccan and Kurdistani people working in the bakery and were messing about making olive oil cakes, which is when we came up with this combination.

**Makes 1 loaf cake**

- 23-cm/9-inch round tin, lined with baking parchment

50g good-quality cocoa powder
2 teaspoons vanilla extract
125ml hot water
200g ground almonds
½ teaspoon bicarbonate of soda
1 teaspoon chilli powder
½ teaspoon fleur de sel de Guérande (or coarse sea salt)
175ml pomace oil (or light virgin olive oil)
3 large eggs
225g unrefined golden caster sugar

Preheat the oven to 200°C/Fan 180°C/Gas 6.

Put the cocoa powder and vanilla extract in a small heatproof bowl, add the hot water and mix into a smooth paste.

In a separate bowl, combine the ground almonds, bicarbonate of soda, chilli powder and salt.

In a large bowl, beat together the pomace oil, eggs and sugar with an electric whisk for 3 minutes until well combined. Gradually whisk in the cocoa powder paste and then fold in the ground almond mixture by hand.

Pour the cake batter into the lined loaf tin and bake for 40 minutes or until it springs back to the touch. Leave the cake in the tin to cool.

When stored in an airtight container in the fridge, this cake will keep for up to 10 days.

# Pineapple, Banana *and* Star Anise Loaf Cake

This cake came about as the result of having a glut of overripe pineapples, which had been given to us by a local greengrocer. Rather than using the juice as a base for a sourdough cake starter as planned, we added chunks of pineapple to a banana base. Instead of the usual combination of ground cinnamon, we tried star anise, which we ground up in a very old spice grinder I have had since my time at Bumblebee. It works wonderfully and tastes like a pineapple upside-down pudding. I highly recommend that you leave the batter overnight as it improves the flavour and thickens it.

**Makes 1 loaf cake**

- 900-g/2-lb loaf tin, lined with baking parchment

4 eggs
170g soft dark brown sugar (or coconut sugar)
80ml pomace oil (or light virgin olive oil)
80g live natural yogurt
175g organic plain wholemeal flour
2 teaspoons ground star anise
1 teaspoon bicarbonate of soda
3 very ripe bananas, mashed
180g ripe pineapple chunks (or tinned chunks)

In a large bowl, beat together the eggs and sugar with an electric whisk until light and creamy. With the whisk running, gradually add the pomace oil in stages and then add the yogurt.

In a separate bowl, combine the flour, ground star anise and bicarbonate of soda.

Fold the flour mixture into the egg mixture using a metal spoon, then fold in the mashed banana and pineapple chunks by hand.

Cover and leave overnight at room temperature.

The next day, preheat the oven to 210°C/Fan 190°C/ Gas 7.

Pour the cake batter into the lined loaf tin and bake for 1 hour or until a sharp knife inserted comes out clean. Leave the cake in the tin to cool.

When stored in an airtight container in the fridge, this cake will keep for 2 weeks.

# Spiced Tea, Sultana *and* Vanilla Buns

We buy little fillable Japanese teabags and add a teaspoon of the spiced tea to a bag so we can use this mix as a standard teabag. It is delicious in warm, creamy oat milk with a dash of vanilla. You can soak the sultanas in the tea for longer if you want – overnight instead of 1 hour – and the dough needs to be left overnight.

**Makes 10 buns**

• 1 large baking tray, lined with baking parchment

2 teaspoons spiced tea mix (see below)
250ml boiling water
125g sultanas
650g organic plain white flour
35g fresh yeast (or 9g dried yeast)
75g golden caster sugar
3 eggs
325ml very cold water
55g salted butter, softened
½ teaspoon fine sea salt
1 tablespoon vanilla extract
2 egg yolks, beaten, for the egg wash

**For the spiced tea mix**
1 cinnamon stick, broken
½ teaspoon whole black peppercorns
½ teaspoon whole pink peppercorns
6 cardamom pods
6 whole cloves

**For the icing**
250g icing sugar, sifted

To make the spiced tea mix, grind all the ingredients to a fine powder in a spice grinder. Place 2 teaspoons of the spiced tea mix into a heatproof jug or bowl and store the rest in an airtight container. Pour on the boiling water and steep for 20 minutes. Strain the tea into a clean bowl. Add the sultanas to the tea and leave to soak overnight (or for 1 hour if you are in a hurry). Drain the sultanas in a sieve and discard the tea.

Place all the other ingredients (except the egg yolks) in the bowl of a mixer with a dough hook. Mix on medium speed for 6 minutes, then add the tea-soaked sultanas and mix for a further 3 minutes to form a smooth dough. Transfer the dough to a bowl, cover completely with food wrap and chill overnight in the fridge.

The next day, divide the dough into 10 equal pieces. Shape each piece into a bun and place on a baking tray lined with baking parchment, spaced 7.5cm/3 inches apart. Cover the tray with a food bag, tie and leave to rise for 2 hours in a warm place.

Preheat the oven to 220°C/Fan 200°C/Gas 7.

Brush the buns liberally with egg wash and bake for 15 minutes or until there is only a little wobble left. Leave the buns on the tray to cool.

To make the icing, mix the icing sugar with just enough warm water to make a thick paste. Spread the top of each bun with icing using the back of a spoon. These buns are best eaten on the same day.

# Tahini, Za'atar *and* Sesame Seed Biscuits

Another accidental discovery, we made these biscuits at the bakehouse when a recipe for a cake we were trying out had tahini added to the sugar instead of honey. Rather than wasting any ingredients, I made biscuits. The first version was not perfect, but the idea inspired me to try again and now everyone loves this sweet and savoury biscuit. It's almost like a cookie as it's quite brittle, and is delicious with a glass of mint tea.

**Makes 28 biscuits**

- 1 large baking tray, lined with baking parchment

150g salted butter, at room temperature

125g soft brown sugar

120g tahini paste

280g organic plain white flour

Zest and juice of 1 organic, unwaxed lemon

½ teaspoon dried mint

1 teaspoon za'atar (see page 176)

25g sesame seeds

45g unrefined golden caster sugar

1 egg, beaten, for the egg wash

Preheat the oven to 200°C/Fan 180°C/Gas 6.

In a bowl, cream together the butter and brown sugar by hand until combined. Add the tahini paste – it might split a little, but do persevere – until everything comes together. Add the flour, lemon zest and juice, dried mint and za'atar and stir until the dough is smooth. Cover the bowl and chill the dough for 30 minutes in the fridge.

In the meantime, toast the sesame seeds in a dry frying pan for 3 minutes – keep the pan moving so the seeds don't burn. Transfer the toasted seeds to a bowl and combine with the caster sugar.

Take the dough out of the fridge and divide equally into 25g pieces. Roll each piece into a smooth ball and place on a lined baking tray. Gently flatten each ball with the back of a spoon. Brush each biscuit with the beaten egg and sprinkle with the sesame seed and sugar mix. Chill for a further 20 minutes in the fridge.

Bake for 15 minutes, keeping a keen eye on the biscuits as they have a tendency to crisp up vigorously round the edges. Leave the biscuits on the tray to cool.

When stored in an airtight container at room temperature, these biscuits will keep for up 7 days. If they start to soften, pop the biscuits back into a hot oven (200°C/Fan 180°C/Gas 6) for 6 minutes.

# Eccles Cakes

I started making Eccles cakes at the request of Jorge Fernandez, when I worked with coffee specialists Fernandez & Wells. My version won the *Evening Standard*'s Best Eccles Cake in London. The pastry is rough puff, but this is my simplified version. As it is a bit of an effort to make, I suggest you make a double quantity of the pastry and then freeze half. You can also make the pastry the night before baking and leave it in the fridge overnight. In the morning, leave the pastry for an hour at room temperature before baking.

**Makes 9 cakes**

• 1 large baking tray, lined
  with baking parchment

**For the pastry**

225g organic strong white
  bread flour

½ teaspoon fine sea salt

200g butter, chilled and cut
  into 2.5-cm/1-inch chunks

175ml ice-cold water

2 egg yolks, beaten, for the
  egg wash

2 tablespoons demerara
  sugar, to sprinkle

**For the filling**

350g currants

150g sultanas

1 teaspoon ground mixed spice

1 organic unwaxed lemon

75g molasses treacle

125g soft brown sugar

4 tablespoons strong breakfast
  tea (or the end of a pot)

**To serve**

Lancashire cheese (such as
  Mrs Kirkham's)

To make the pastry, sift the flour into a bowl and add the salt and butter. Making sure your hands are cold, rub the butter into the flour for 2 minutes – at this point, pieces of butter should still be very visible. Add the cold water and gently bring the mixture together quickly to form a stiff dough. Cover with food wrap and leave to chill for 30 minutes in the fridge.

Place the dough on a lightly floured surface and knead for 3 minutes. Using a rolling pin, shape the dough into a 40 x 20-cm/16 x 8-inch rectangle. You should still be able to see streaks of butter through the dough.

Take the top third of the dough and fold it into the centre. Next, take the bottom third of the dough and do the same. Now fold the two sides of the dough in to look like a book. Repeat this process one more time. Cover with food wrap and leave to chill for 2 hours in the fridge before using.

Meanwhile, place all the ingredients for the filling in the bowl of a mixer with the paddle attachment. Make sure the guard is on the machine or you might have a kitchen full of flying currants. Mix on medium speed for 10 minutes or until the ingredients form a paste.

Preheat the oven to 240°C/Fan 220°C/Gas 9.

Working quickly so that the pastry does not warm up, roll out the dough into a 30-cm/12-inch square and cut

evenly into nine 10-cm/4-inch squares. Spoon 80g of the filling into the centre of each pastry square.

With one square in the palm of your hand, draw up each side of the pastry over the filling and seal over the centre of the fruit. Flip the pastry parcel over and place it, seam-side down, on a lined baking tray. Repeat with the other squares.

Gently push down on each cake with the palm of your hand and then brush them liberally all over with the egg wash. Using a small sharp knife, make three short parallel cuts in the centre of each pastry parcel and sprinkle with the demerara sugar.

Bake for 25 minutes until the cakes are well browned and the filling is bubbling through the little cuts. Leave the cakes on the tray to cool. Serve with a wedge of Lancashire cheese.

When stored in an airtight container, these cakes will keep for 5 days.

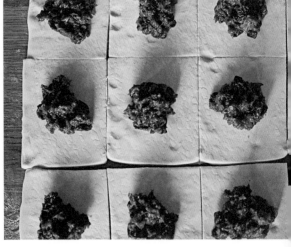

# Bread-ish

An enriched dough is basically a cross between a bread and a cake –
richer than a bread because milk or butter has been added, but less
sweet than a cake. If you go on to ferment that enriched dough, you
get an amazing flavour, but there's no need for complicated recipes
with fiddly stages. Everyone assumes that my batbout buns (see
page 130) are a sourdough, but it's a quick bread mix that's been
enriched with yogurt to give it that distinctive tang. I want to make
this chapter super enjoyable for you by keeping things simple – and
with a brilliant end result.

In this chapter, you will find the most bread-like of my bakes, enriched
with butter, yogurt or buttermilk. Some of these recipes also have
sweet notes and I add fruit and spices as well as sugar to brioche. There
are two base recipes – the first is my soda bread base (see page 122),
which is a drier, breadier mix; the second is my brioche base (see page
135), which is, uniquely, an all-in-one mix.

Soda bread is traditionally made with soured milk (buttermilk) as my
grandmother did. She literally left her milk out in a glass bottle on the
kitchen windowsill, sometimes in the summer sun, until it was stinky.
Nowadays, people use commercially made buttermilk or thin live
yogurt. You can add anything you want to this soda bread base really,
but you need an activator for the bicarbonate of soda so you can't use
oat milk. If you can't get hold of buttermilk, you can just add a little
lemon juice to milk (there is a recipe for this on page 180). I remember
that people used to add white pepper and salt to milk and then drink
it, but I have no idea why …

Although I do have a background in pâtisserie, my brioche base is
not the classic but tricky dough that you will see pâtisserie chefs
making. When I started selling my bakes to cafés, I soon found
shortcuts to make a brioche dough without having to go through lots
of complicated steps. People can get very particular about brioche
because traditionally the dough is made in stages with the cold butter
added in slowly at the end. My method mixes everything together but
then I leave the dough in the fridge for 3 days. It makes for a heavier
dough, more like a bread than the softer brioche texture, but it still
rises beautifully.

The morning buns (see pages 136–146) use the same simple brioche dough as their base, but are then filled in different ways. The sugar-topped bun is the simplest. For a savoury baked brioche, just take the top off the bun, add an egg yolk and put it back in the oven, then top with chimichurri. The others are baked with a custard top or filled like a doughnut, while for the chocolate bun the dough is dotted with chocolate buttons before baking. For a really glorious finish, use egg yolks with a deep yellow colour, like those from St. Ewe's.

As I write, we are now making a very simple organic sourdough bread. It's not something I planned for Fortitude, but due to COVID we have had to adapt to the lockdowns of the past months. We don't have provers or a deck oven at the bakehouse, but we are very good at making-do – I made a tent with a small heater tucked inside to prove bread. I have made Italian socca, Ethiopian flatbreads and Moroccan khobz and I love using alternative flours like chickpea and teff as well as einkorn, semolina and potato.

My many visits to Morocco and to my Moroccan family always inspired my baking and cooking. The way they made bread, squatting on the floor, mixing the dough by hand in a large, oily wide-brimmed terracotta plate. The bread would be made, shaped and proved at home and then taken down the road to the communal oven to bake, alongside bread from many other families. I loved watching all the trays covered in their family cloths, sitting atop heads, weaving their way through the medina. Baffled by how the communal oven man remembered whose bread was whose, when I asked, he said he knew the hands of the bakers, and Rachid said that they very rarely got the wrong bread back – if they did, it would be cause for much gossip and comparison. Best of all, though, was the fact that the oven's fires also heated the water for the communal hammams.

Bread-ish

# Sour Milk Soda Bread

I make soda bread, as opposed to sourdough or yeasted bread, because I grew up eating it every day. My grandmother made the most wonderful soda bread using milk left to turn sour and baked it in a heavy, black cooking pot that hung over the open fire. The sour milk produced a tangy concoction that, as a child, I would run from the smell of, but never connected to the delicious bread, butter and jam served up at the kitchen table daily at 4pm with china cups full of strong tea. The bread tasted smoky and sour, but my grandfather called it sweet cake or currant cake if a handful of dried fruit had been added. For my soda bread, I use a mixture of buttermilk and live yogurt. I like to use probiotic live yogurt because it's sour, mellow and very healthy. It also gives my soda bread a really soft crumb because yogurt reacts better with the soda than either milk or buttermilk. Everyone remarks on how soft and cakey my soda bread is at Fortitude.

**Makes 1 × 500-g round loaf**

• 1 baking tray, lightly floured

500g organic plain white flour
1½ teaspoons bicarbonate
  of soda
1 teaspoon fine sea salt
250ml buttermilk
  (see page 180)
150g live natural yogurt

Preheat the oven to 220°C/Fan 200°C/Gas 7.

Sift together the flour, bicarbonate of soda and salt in a large bowl. Make a well in the centre and add the buttermilk and yogurt. Bring all the ingredients together until just combined, but do not overmix – if you overwork soda bread dough it becomes pudding-like and the bread doesn't rise. The dough should be soft, not too wet and just a little bit sticky.

When the dough has come together, place it on a floured baking tray and shape into a round that is 5cm/2 inches deep. Cut the traditional cross shape into the bread, cutting quite deep – to within about 1cm/½ inch from the bottom – so that the loaf retains the cross shape while baking. Lightly dust with flour.

Bake for 35–40 minutes or until the bread sounds hollow, like a drum, when tapped on the base.

When stored in an airtight container, this soda bread and all the offshoots that follow will keep for 2 days. If toasted, you will get another day's use.

When I first started baking I was always experimenting with the traditional recipes that were part of my family's daily life – at the age of 14, my favourite line was 'let's just jazz it up'. I am sure not all of my jazzing up was successful, but my grandparents never complained and always made me feel like my baking was the best in the world. I am continually searching for new variations and take inspiration from meals eaten in restaurants or my fellow bakers at Fortitude. Here are some of the offshoots to my grandmother's original soda bread recipe that I still make today.

### Red Wine-Soaked Raisin Soda Bread

*Here, red wine adds tartness to the dried fruit, which needs an overnight soak before baking. This loaf is wonderful served with cheese, or toasted and eaten with pâté, terrine or rillettes and a side of salted, fermented butter.*

150g raisins
150ml good-quality, natural red wine

Put the raisins in a small bowl and pour over the red wine. Leave to soak overnight.

When ready to bake, make the soda bread dough following the instructions on page 122, adding the raisin and wine mixture along with the other wet ingredients – the dough might be a strange mauve colour. Shape and bake the loaf as instructed on page 122.

### Tomato, Garlic and Oregano Soda Bread

*I really like dried oregano and I use a lot of it at the bakehouse – it's my go-to herb.*

6 medium tomatoes, halved
4 garlic cloves, peeled and crushed
4 tablespoons olive oil
½ teaspoon dried oregano
½ teaspoon fine sea salt
150g fontina cheese, grated

Preheat the oven to 220°C/Fan 200°C/Gas 7.

Place the tomatoes and garlic on a baking tray and drizzle with the olive oil. Sprinkle with the dried oregano and salt then roast in the hot oven for 10 minutes.

When ready to bake, make the soda bread dough following the instructions on page 122. Press out the dough to 2.5cm/1 inch thick, then pile on the tomatoes and garlic, together with any oil from the tray. Bake the loaf in the hot oven for 15 minutes, then scatter over the cheese and return to the oven for a further 15 minutes.

## Marmalade Soda Bread

*When my baking obsession started as a teenager, my mother suggested that I add a jar of her marmalade (which she made every January) to a soda-bread mix. This makes for the best-ever toast with built-in marmalade – just spread with salty butter for a breakfast treat. The dough is sticky and a little hard to handle, so flour your hands well when shaping the loaf.*

250g jar Seville orange marmalade
  (see page 181)

Make the soda bread dough following the instructions on page 122, adding the marmalade along with the other wet ingredients. Shape and bake the loaf as instructed on page 122.

## Orange and Raisin Soda Bread

*Inspired by making soda bread scones, but with raisins added to that mix.*

150g raisins
Zest and juice of 1 organic,
  unwaxed orange

Put the raisins and orange zest in a small bowl and pour over the orange juice. Leave to soak for 1 hour.

When ready to bake, make the soda bread dough following the instructions on page 122, adding the raisin and orange mixture along with the other wet ingredients. Shape and bake the loaf as instructed on page 122.

## Chocolate and Prune Soda Bread

*Here's a sweet variation. The chocolate and prunes (which are soaked overnight in Cointreau) give a deeper, richer note to the tangy base recipe, good for a late brunch or afternoon pick-me-up.*

200g prunes
150ml Cointreau orange liqueur
250g dark chocolate, chopped

Put the prunes in a small bowl and pour over the orange liqueur. Leave to soak overnight.

When ready to bake, finely chop the soaked prunes and make the soda bread dough following the instructions on page 122, adding the chopped chocolate and prunes along with the other dry ingredients. Shape and bake the loaf, as instructed on page 122.

## Blue Cheese, Pear and Walnut Soda Bread

*This is delicious with charcuterie. This loaf is cooked at a higher temperature than the previous soda breads because it needs a harder crust due to the soft cheese.*

85g shelled walnuts
2 very ripe pears, peeled, cored and
  cut into 1-cm/½-inch pieces
150g Cashel blue cheese, cut into 1-cm/
  ½-inch pieces

Preheat the oven to 200°C/Fan 180°C/ Gas 6.

Spread the walnuts over a baking tray and toast in the oven for 5 minutes. Once cool, roughly chop.

Increase the oven temperature to 220°C/ Fan 200°C/Gas 7.

Make the soda bread dough following the instructions on page 122, adding the toasted walnuts to the other dry ingredients and the pear pieces with the other wet ingredients.

Once the dough has come together, place it on a lightly floured surface. Work the cheese through the dough, though not too vigorously as the cheese should be baked into the crust. Shape the loaf as instructed on page 122. Bake the loaf for 30 minutes or until it sounds hollow, like a drum, when tapped on the base.

## Cheddar, Sultana and Carrot Pickle Soda Bread

*This soda bread offshoot was inspired by a favourite cheese scone recipe. At the bakehouse, we make this soda bread in winter and serve it with our soups.*

150g Cheddar cheese, grated
  (I mainly use Montgomery Cheddar)
100g sultanas
100g carrot pickle, finely chopped
  (or any other hard vegetable pickle)

When ready to bake, make the soda bread dough following the instructions on page 122, adding the cheese, sultanas and chopped pickle along with the other dry ingredients. Shape and bake the loaf as instructed on page 122.

# Batbout Buns *with* Berber Omelette

A batbout is a soft breakfast bread made in Morocco with white flour, sometimes coarse semolina and always dried yeast. I make mine with organic self-raising flour, yogurt and a pinch of salt. Each day at the bakehouse, I make batbout in homage to my wonderful daughters Soumiya and Sophia, who bring light to my eyes. When Soumiya was eight and Sophia was four years old, I took them on a three-month trip to Marrakech as I wanted them to have memories of their Moroccan family and culture – I know these memories have never left them and have been formative in their lives. We had driven four hours out of Marrakech, up into the High Atlas mountains, when Sophia declared she was starving – when that happened, believe me, something had to be done. We stopped on a pass overlooking the vast valley below where there happened to be a small galvanised metal hut. Inside was an elderly gentleman who approached me to chat, as Moroccans love to do. He told us he was a Berber who had lived on the High Atlas mountains all of his life. On hearing Sophia was hungry he went back into his little dwelling and ten minutes later returned with the most delicious omelette made with green pepper and ground cumin on a piece of Moroccan flatbread, all doused in olive oil.

**For the batbout buns
(makes 5 buns)**
250g organic self-raising white flour
1 teaspoon sea salt
250g live natural yogurt

**For the Berber omelette
(makes 1 omelette)**
1 tablespoon olive oil
½ small onion, thinly sliced
½ teaspoon ground cumin
½ teaspoon ground coriander
2 eggs, beaten well
½ teaspoon finely chopped mint
½ teaspoon finely chopped coriander
¼ teaspoon fine sea salt

Preheat the oven to 220°C/Fan 200°C/Gas 7.

To make the batbout buns, sift the flour and salt into a bowl. Add the yogurt and bring everything together using your hands until well combined and there is no flour visible.

Divide the dough into 5 x 100-g balls and flatten them by hand into 10-cm/4-inch rounds. Batbout buns are meant to be rustic, so do not get caught up with using a rolling pin or trying to shape them perfectly.

Place the rounds on a lined baking tray and bake for 8 minutes, flipping them over halfway through the cooking time.

Meanwhile, preheat a ridged grill pan. Take the buns out of the oven and place each one on the preheated grill. Check after 2 minutes and when the buns have those blackened grill lines, flip them over to achieve the same effect on the other side.

To make the Berber omelette, heat the olive oil in a heavy-based frying pan. Add the onion and fry for 3 minutes. Add the spices and cook over a low heat for a further 5 minutes, then add the beaten eggs, chopped herbs and salt. This is not like a traditional omelette so you can vigorously stir the mixture until just cooked.

Split open a batbout bun and pack in the omelette. We serve ours with a tablespoon of spicy harissa on top of the omelette.

Bread-ish

I created this recipe because I wanted something lovely for breakfast without having to get up early and spend hours faffing about making dough. I now make this base mix in vast quantities as we sell lots of brioche morning buns at the bakehouse. The method is unconventional: it is not made in the French-style where butter is added in bits at end. My method will not work if you do that (I have had bakers take it upon themselves to change the method and can't quite figure out why it hasn't worked for them). With this recipe, you make the dough and leave it overnight, then bake either the whole batch or only what you need for breakfast in the morning. For me, the key to this brioche is the eggs – they must be rich yellow yolks, and preferably organic.

**Makes 2 small loaves or 10 buns**

- 2 × 450-g/1-lb loaf tins greased well with oil or 1 baking tray, lined with baking parchment

600g organic plain white flour
15g fresh yeast (or 9g dried yeast)
6 eggs with rich yellow yolks
45g unrefined organic sugar
225g salted butter, at room temperature
1 teaspoon fine sea salt

**For the egg wash**
2 eggs with rich yellow yolks, beaten

Place the flour, yeast, eggs, sugar, butter and salt in the bowl of a mixer fitted with a dough hook. Mix on medium speed for 8 minutes.

Once combined, place the dough in a container and cover with food wrap. Leave to rest at room temperature for 30 minutes and then chill in the fridge overnight.

When ready to bake, take the dough out of the fridge. For loaves, divide it into 6 x 200-g balls. Put 3 balls into each greased loaf tin so that they fit snugly. Cover the tins with a clean tea towel and leave to rest in a warm place for 1 hour (or 3 hours in fridge for a slower rise). For buns, follow the shaping instructions on page 136.

Preheat the oven to 220°C/Fan 200°C/Gas 7.

Brush the loaves or buns liberally all over with the egg wash. Bake the loaves for 30 minutes and the buns for 20 minutes or until golden brown on top. Leave the loaves in the tin and the buns on the tray to cool.

TO FERMENT
Store the brioche dough for up to 3 days in the fridge.

When stored in an airtight container, the baked brioche will keep for 3 days. When stale, use it for French toast.

# Brioche Buns
# *with* Sugar Top

This comes from my classical French training where the brioche is topped with crystallised sugar lumps. These are delicious eaten warm with butter and jam.

**Makes 10 buns**

• 1 baking tray, lined with
  baking parchment

1 quantity of simple brioche
  dough (see page 135)
2 eggs with rich yellow yolks,
  beaten, for the egg wash
Demerara sugar, to sprinkle

When ready to bake, take the dough out of the fridge and divide it into 10 x 100-g balls or as many 100-g balls as needed (you can keep the rest in the fridge.)

Leave the dough balls to sit for 10 minutes. To shape the buns, roll the balls over a lightly floured surface until smooth: make a cup shape with your hand, place it over the ball without applying too much pressure and move it continuously in a circular motion for 15 seconds. Roll again into a 10-cm/4-inch round that is almost flat.

Place each round on a lined baking tray, spaced 2.5cm/1 inch apart. Set aside to rest in a warm place for 1 hour.

Preheat the oven to 220°C/Fan 200°C/Gas 7.

Brush the buns liberally all over with the egg wash and sprinkle liberally with the sugar. Bake the buns for 20 minutes or until golden brown on top. Leave the buns on the baking tray to cool for 10 minutes. Serve warm.

# Chocolate *and* Brown Sugar Brioche Buns

The Rapha cyclists are great friends of Fortitude and stop by on sunny mornings to fill up on buns and coffee. Aleda, the ride organiser, always gives us a heads up when they are on their way. One time after she called, we realised that we had no cinnamon buns or brioche buns. As we always have our simple brioche dough in the fridge, we quickly rolled out some buns with chocolate chips and brown sugar. They emerged from the oven like molten monsters and they are now a regular fixture on our menu.

**Makes 10 buns**

- 1 baking tray, lined with baking parchment

1 quantity of simple brioche dough (see page 135)
250g dark chocolate buttons
2 tablespoons soft brown sugar
2 eggs with rich yellow yolks, beaten, for the egg wash

When ready to bake, take the dough out of the fridge and add the chocolate buttons and brown sugar. Place the dough back into the bowl of a mixer fitted with a dough hook mix on medium speed for 3 minutes.

Divide the dough into 10 x 100-g balls or as many 100-g balls as needed (you can keep the rest in the fridge).

Leave the dough balls to sit for 10 minutes. To shape the buns, roll the balls over a lightly floured surface until smooth: make a cup shape with your hand, place it over the ball without applying too much pressure and move it continuously in a circular motion for 15 seconds. Roll again into a 10-cm/4-inch round that is almost flat.

Place each round on a lined baking tray, spaced 2.5cm/1 inch apart. Set aside to rest in a warm place for 1 hour.

Preheat the oven to 200°C/Fan 180°C/Gas 6.

Brush the buns liberally all over with the egg wash. Bake the buns for 20 minutes or until golden brown on top. Leave the buns on the baking tray to cool.

*From left to right:* Chocolate and Brown Sugar Brioche Bun, Sticky Apple Morning Brioche Bun, Brioche Bun with Sugar Top, Turmeric Custard and Roast Pear Brioche Bun, Simple Brioche Bun.

Bread-ish

# Brioche Buns *with* Blackberry *and* Cardamom Syrup

The blackberries are a nod to when we used to fraughan when we were kids. This means to forage in Irish – it was bilberries if you were in the north or blackberries in the south.

**Makes 10 buns**

• 1 baking tray, lined with baking parchment

1 quantity of simple brioche dough (see page 135)
2 eggs with rich yellow yolks, beaten, for the egg wash
Caster sugar, to sprinkle
Vanilla ice cream, to serve
Icing sugar, to dust

**For the blackberry syrup**
250g blackberries
2 tablespoons unrefined golden caster sugar
1 teaspoon ground cardamom
50ml water

When ready to bake, take the dough out of the fridge and divide it into 10 x 100-g balls or as many 100-g balls as needed (you can keep the rest in the fridge).

Leave the dough balls to sit for 10 minutes. To shape the buns, roll the balls over a lightly floured surface until smooth: make a cup shape with your hand, place it over the ball without applying too much pressure and move it continuously in a circular motion for 15 seconds. Roll again into a 10-cm/4-inch round that is almost flat.

Place each round on a lined baking tray, spaced 2.5cm/1 inch apart. Set aside to rest in a warm place for 1 hour.

Meanwhile, make the blackberry syrup. Place the blackberries, caster sugar, cardamom and water in a pan and cook over a low heat for 10 minutes or until the blackberries start to bubble. Remove from the heat and leave to sit until the brioche buns are baked.

Preheat the oven to 220°C/Fan 200°C/Gas 7.

Brush the buns liberally all over with the egg wash and sprinkle lightly with sugar. Bake the buns for 18 minutes or until golden brown on top. Leave the buns on the baking tray to cool for 5 minutes.

Cut each bun in half and spoon the blackberries and syrup over the bottom of the brioche bun. Add a scoop of vanilla ice cream, then place the brioche bun top back on and dust with icing sugar.

# Turmeric Custard *and* Roast Pear Brioche Buns

Adding turmeric to custard was inspired by my travels around Morocco, where they use turmeric in sweet as well as savoury dishes. We were making custard one day at Fortitude and one batch of egg yolks had no colour. I considered using saffron to make the custard more yellow but then I remembered what I had seen in Morocco.

**Makes 10 buns**

- 1 baking tray, lined with baking parchment

1 quantity of simple brioche dough (see page 135)
2 eggs with rich yellow yolks, beaten, for the egg wash
280g flaked almonds

**For the roast pears**
3 pears, cored and cut into quarters
4 tablespoons caster sugar
2 teaspoons ground cinnamon
1 tablespoon butter

**For the turmeric custard**
4 egg yolks
75g brown sugar
55g organic plain white flour
½ teaspoon ground turmeric
300ml full-fat milk, brought to the boil and left to cool to warm

When ready to bake, take the dough out of the fridge and divide into 10 x 100-g balls or as many 100-g balls as needed (you can keep the rest in the fridge).

Leave the dough balls to sit for 10 minutes. To shape the buns roll the balls over a lightly floured surface until smooth: make a cup shape with your hand, place it over the ball without applying too much pressure and move it continuously in a circular motion for 15 seconds. Roll again into a 10-cm/4-inch round that is almost flat.

Place each round on a lined baking tray, spaced 2.5cm/1 inch apart. Set aside to rest in a warm place for 1 hour.

Preheat the oven to 220°C/Fan 200°C/Gas 7.

To roast the pears, toss the pear quarters in the sugar and cinnamon. Lay them in a baking dish and dot with the butter. Bake for 15 minutes or until caramelised.

To make the custard, combine the egg yolks, sugar, flour and turmeric in a bowl to form a smooth paste. Pour over the warm milk, whisking continuously. Transfer the mixture to a pan and cook over a medium heat, stirring all the time, until it thickens. Place in a container and put a piece of food wrap directly on the surface of the custard to stop a skin forming. Leave to cool. This custard will keep refrigerated for 5 days.

Reduce the oven temperature to 200°C/Fan 180°C/Gas 6.

Top each bun with a tablespoon of the turmeric custard and a piece or two of roast pear.

Brush the buns liberally with the egg wash and sprinkle with the flaked almonds. Bake the buns for 18 minutes or until golden brown on top. Leave the buns on the baking tray to cool for 10 minutes. Serve warm.

# Chimichurri Brioche Buns

We make chimichurri brioche buns regularly at the bakehouse. One of the bakers, Tom, suggested topping the brioche with a rich, yellow, organic egg yolk. We now have the perfect breakfast bun.

**Makes 10 buns**

- 1 baking tray, lined with baking parchment

1 quantity of simple brioche dough (see page 135)
2 eggs with rich yellow yolks, beaten, for the egg wash
1 egg yolk per bun

**For the chimichurri**
1 shallot, finely chopped
1 red chilli, finely chopped
3 garlic cloves, crushed
1 large bunch of coriander, chopped
1 small bunch of mint, chopped
1 teaspoon dried thyme
250ml olive oil

When ready to bake, take the dough out of the fridge and divide it into 10 x 100-g balls or as many 100-g balls as needed (you can keep the rest in the fridge).

Leave the dough balls to sit for 10 minutes. To shape the buns, roll the balls over a lightly floured surface until smooth: cup your hand, place it over the ball without applying too much pressure and move it continuously in a circular motion for 15 seconds. Roll again into a 10-cm/4-inch round that is almost flat.

Place each round on a lined baking tray, spaced 2.5cm/1 inch apart, and brush liberally all over with egg wash. Leave to rest at room temperature for 20 minutes.

Preheat the oven to 200°C/Fan 180°C/Gas 6.

Meanwhile, make the chimichurri. Combine all the ingredients in a jar and give it a good shake. (This mix keeps well in the fridge for 2 weeks so you can keep any leftover to use in other dishes or when you want to make more buns.)

Bake the buns for 18 minutes or until golden brown on top. Leave the buns on the sheet to cool for 10 minutes.

Once cool enough to handle, cut out a 2.5-cm/1-inch circle about 2cm/¾ inch deep from the top of each bun. (You can make breadcrumbs with the offcuts, so do not discard them.)

Place an egg yolk in each hole made in the buns, put them back in the oven and bake for 4 minutes. Remove from the oven and spoon over a tablespoon of the chimichurri. Serve warm.

# Sticky Apple Morning Brioche Buns

Back in Ireland my family only ever really marked Easter and Christmas, although we did bob for apples at Hallowe'en from a plastic washing up bowl brimming with fruit. Over the days that followed, we enjoyed apple pie and stewed apple with rice or tapioca thickened with buttermilk. These are our Hallowe'en buns at the bakehouse.

**Makes 10 buns**

- 1 baking tray, lined with baking parchment

1 quantity of simple brioche dough (see page 135)
2 eggs with rich yellow yolks, beaten, for the egg wash
5 teaspoons demerara sugar

**For the spiced apple**
4 cooking apples, peeled and chopped into 2.5-cm/1-inch cubes
4 tablespoons brown sugar
1 teaspoon ground cinnamon
100ml double cream

To make the spiced apple, place the chopped apples in a pan with the sugar and cinnamon. Cook over a medium heat for 15 minutes or until the apple is almost cooked down. Stir in the double cream.

When ready to bake, take the dough out of the fridge and divide it into 10 x 100-g balls or as many 100-g balls as needed (you can keep the rest in the fridge).

Leave the dough balls to sit for 10 minutes. To shape the buns, roll over a lightly floured surface until smooth: make a cup shape with your hand, place it over the ball without applying too much pressure and move it continuously in a circular motion for 15 seconds. Roll again into a 10-cm/4-inch round that is almost flat.

Preheat the oven to 200°C/Fan 180°C/Gas 6.

Place a tablespoon of the spiced apple in the centre of each round, bring the dough up around the apple and pinch to seal – almost as if you were making a dumpling. Turn the buns over and place seam-side down on a lined baking tray.

Brush the buns liberally all over with the egg wash and leave for 10 minutes. Sprinkle ½ teaspoon sugar over the top of each bun. Bake the buns for 20 minutes or until golden brown on top. Leave the buns on the baking tray to cool for 10 minutes. Serve warm.

# Cinnamon Brioche
## *with* Honey Marzipan

Over 20 years ago, I started making bostock at Bumblebee because our Canadian chef Suzanne needed to make French toast. She would take a slice of brioche with half and half, or single cream, and a beaten egg and then soak it in syrup and bake it with frangipane to make bostock. I needed a way to make a brioche loaf interesting for Fortitude, so I did a kind of bostock and put bits of honey marzipan in to make it less bready. Like the brioche base, this dough needs to be left overnight in the fridge.

**Makes 2 small loaves**

- 2 × 450-g/1-lb loaf tins greased well with pomace oil

600g organic plain white flour
15g fresh yeast (or 9g dried yeast)
6 eggs
45g unrefined organic sugar
225g salted butter, at room temperature
1 teaspoon fine sea salt
2 teaspoons ground cinnamon
200g honey marzipan (see page 184), cut into 1-cm/ ½-inch pieces
2 eggs with rich yellow yolks, beaten, for the egg wash

Place the flour, yeast, eggs, sugar, butter, salt, cinnamon and honey marzipan in the bowl of a mixer fitted with a dough hook. Mix on medium speed for 8 minutes.

Once well combined, place the dough in a plastic container and cover with food wrap. Leave to rest at room temperature for 30 minutes and then chill in the fridge overnight.

When ready to bake, take the dough out of the fridge and divide it into 6 x 200-g balls. Put 3 balls into each greased loaf tin so that they fit snugly. Cover the loaf tins with a clean tea towel and leave to rest in a warm place for 1 hour (or 3 hours in fridge if you want to it rise slowly).

Preheat the oven to 220°C/Fan 200°C/Gas 7.

Brush the loaves liberally all over with the egg wash. Bake the loaves for 30 minutes or until golden brown on top. Leave the loaves in the tin to cool.

# Candied Orange Sourdough Hot Cross Buns

We make these every Easter in huge quantities so I wanted a simple recipe that we can prepare one day, refrigerate, then bake the next. I use mixed peel in this recipe but we also use equal amounts of sultanas and raisins too. You will need the buttermilk starter (days 1–4) from the Sourdough and Fermented Cakes chapter (see page 154) and the dough is left overnight in the fridge.

**Makes 12 buns**

- 1 baking tray, lined with baking parchment

**For the buns**
300g organic plain white flour
150g organic wholemeal flour
200ml warm water
65ml pomace oil (or light virgin olive oil)
3 tablespoons ground mixed spice
110g buttermilk starter (see page 154)
1 teaspoon fine sea salt
150g mixed peel, finely chopped
2 eggs, beaten, for the egg wash
Warmed apricot jam, to glaze

**For the crosses**
3 tablespoons organic plain white flour
85g warm water

To make the buns, put all the ingredients except the mixed peel, eggs and jam into the bowl of a mixer fitted with a dough hook. Mix on medium speed for 8 minutes or until the dough is shiny and elastic.

Transfer the dough to a lightly floured surface and gently flatten into a disc. Cover the disc with the chopped peel and knead it gently into the dough by hand for 5 minutes, making sure the peel is evenly distributed. Place the dough in a lightly oiled container and cover with food wrap. Leave to rest in the fridge overnight.

The next day, divide the dough into 12 equal pieces. Roll out into balls and place on a lined baking tray. Cover and leave to rest at room temperature for 2 hours or until the balls have at least doubled in size and have plenty of give when lightly pressed.

To make the paste for the crosses, vigorously mix the flour with the warm water to form a paste and transfer it to a piping bag. Brush the buns liberally with the egg wash and then pipe the paste in the shape of a cross on top of each one. Leave to rest for a further 30 minutes.

Preheat the oven to 200°C/Fan 180°C/Gas 6.

Bake the buns for 22–25 minutes or until well browned on top. While still warm, glaze the buns by lightly brushing them with a little warmed apricot jam.

# Sourdough *and* Fermented Cakes

There are two key stages to making the cakes in this chapter: firstly, making a starter and secondly, fermenting the cake batter itself. These distinct steps – the processes I talk about in the introduction to this book – form the essence of my craft baking and are the basis of everything I do at Fortitude. This process of making a cake does take a week in total, but I want you to view it as integral to the craft of baking. As you observe the fermentation process over the days, you will come to understand what is happening to your bakes. There's no extra effort involved – all you need to do is leave them be. I love watching a cake batter develop over the days and, however many times I do this, there's always a surprise and sometimes a new idea.

The milk-based starter will help your cake to rise but also give it a tremendous nutty flavour. All you do is mix buttermilk, flour and sugar over four days (that's really all you do) and then, for the first set of recipes, add in a simple butter cake mix of flour, unrefined sugar, eggs and butter – and ground almonds, which activate the starter (you can also use banana or pineapple juice) that you ferment for three days. I also use a raising agent, self-raising flour. The starter is dairy based, so you can't keep feeding it like a sourdough starter, though you can freeze it. That's the basic recipe and then you can add whatever you want to it – I've given five variations here, but I want you to go ahead and experiment as I did. You'll come to learn what works and what doesn't. You'll end up with a giant buttery cake, rather like a Madeleine, that will last for a week.

Fermenting a batter simply means leaving your cake mixture to sit for three days before you bake it. There is no additional work required, you just need a little patience and to plan ahead if you want to make this cake for an occasion. In return, you will enjoy a far more interesting cake because the fermentation leads to a more complex flavour and texture (like sourdough bread).

Fermentation is a fascinating process. At some point, you will doubtless question whether it really will work, so let me reassure you. The fermented cake batter is a loose, liquid mix, even at the point of putting it in the oven, and especially in warmer weather. Trust the process and, most important of all, have some fun. Watch the liquid bubbling up and the smell is just phenomenal, especially the banana ferment.

My banana and bilberry sourdough loaf cake (see page 164) was the first bake I made following this fermentation method. When I started, I left a tub of banana ferment out for seven days, kind of like a science experiment. It was summer and the mix basically became a magic pudding – it just grew and grew. It still uses a raising agent (bicarbonate of soda) but even though you are taught to bake a cake as soon as the bicarbonate of soda has been added because it loses power over time, I have found you can leave the mix for up to a week. The banana cake in this chapter rises like a massive loaf of bread. You also can't refrigerate these ferments, but equally they don't like hot temperatures. I never make the Guinness cake when it's really hot because the bicarbonate of soda reacts like honeycomb.

You will find that these cakes will keep for a week or so and are really versatile. They have a cakey texture, but you can slice and toast them just like bread and eat them spread with butter or serve them as a dessert with cream and fruit – either way, they taste amazing.

My final and best reason for fermenting cakes and making starters is because I believe that wild yeast (which is why I say to mix the batter with your hands) and fermented foods have so many health benefits for your body. If you're going to make a cake, it should be the best cake possible, not just for flavour but nutritionally too, so go on and bake – it's good for you!

Sourdough and Fermented Cakes

# Buttermilk Starter
## *for* Sourdough Loaf Cakes

The main cakes we make at the bakery every day are sourdough loaf cakes. We love this cake, as do our many customers. It is a dense, buttery cake that can be eaten as is, served with jam, fried in butter with maple syrup, or made into a trifle. You need to start the process well in advance of baking, but there is actually very little work to do – it's an easy cake to make, you just need a bit of patience. Making the cake is a two-part process. First, you create a sourdough starter from buttermilk that is fed and grows over 4 days. Then you make the butter cake mix (see page 156), to which you add this buttermilk starter and leave to ferment for 3 days before baking.

**Makes enough for 1 loaf cake**

• 2-litre preserving jar with a
lid that does not fit too snugly

**For each day 1–4**
80ml buttermilk
(see page 180)
25g organic self-raising
white flour
25g unrefined golden
caster sugar

*Day 1*
Combine all the ingredients in a bowl and mix everything together using your hands. Always use your hands for mixing as the naturally occurring yeast on your skin helps to kickstart the fermentation process.

Transfer the starter mixture to the preserving jar, but don't seal it tightly as you need some naturally occurring bacteria to get in there to feed your starter. Leave the jar somewhere cool, but not in the fridge (unless it's very hot weather, in which case, refrigerate).

*Day 2*
Top up the preserving jar with the buttermilk, flour and sugar, and mix again using your hands.

*Day 3*
Repeat the process from the previous day. After the third day, the starter should be a little bit bubbly and smell slightly nutty.

*Day 4*
Repeat the process from the previous days.

# Sourdough Butter Cake Base Mix

This butter cake is the most pared-back sourdough cake I make. This recipe – and the others that follow – uses the buttermilk starter from page 154, but has its own fermented cake mix. Start at least the day before you want to bake as you need to leave the cake batter overnight, but it can be fermented for longer. This cake is unadorned so you get to appreciate the flavour and texture of the sourdough itself; however, I often vary the flavours and have included recipe offshoots on pages 157–162. I use self-raising flour, but you can use plain: it does not give the same rise, but still tastes beautiful. I recommend making a double quantity of this sourdough butter cake base mix as, once fermented, it keeps for up to 10 days or the cooked loaf cakes can be frozen, if need be.

**Makes 1 loaf cake**

- Plastic container with lid
- 900-g/2-lb loaf tin, lined with baking parchment, floured and buttered (do not use oil as it affects the starter)

200g salted butter, softened
200g soft light brown sugar
4 eggs
225g organic self-raising white flour
50g ground almonds
150g buttermilk starter (see page 154)

### Day 1
Place the butter and sugar in the bowl of a mixer fitted with a paddle attachment and mix together on medium speed for 5 minutes or until light and creamy. Add the eggs one at a time and continue to mix until combined, but do not overmix. In a separate bowl, combine the flour and ground almonds. Fold the flour and almond mixture into the creamed butter in three batches. Fold in the buttermilk starter using your hands. Transfer the cake batter to a plastic container and seal with a lid. Store the container at room temperature for 2–3 days. During this time, the batter will ferment and become runny and bubbly.

### Day 3
When ready to bake, preheat the oven to 200°C/Fan 180°C/Gas 6. Before you use the cake batter, fold it over again using your hands until smooth. Pour the cake batter into the lined, floured and buttered loaf tin. Wrap the tin loosely in baking parchment, like a cocoon, to prevent tiny volcanic explosions from the centre. Bake for 1 hour 15 minutes or until a sharp knife inserted into the centre of the cake comes out clean.

When wrapped in waxed paper and stored in an airtight container, this loaf cake will keep for 7 days.

Any of the following flavours can be added to the sourdough butter cake base mix on Day 3. These additional ingredients can only be introduced to the cake batter after it has been fermenting for three days, otherwise they will affect the action of the starter as it ferments.

## Moroccan Honey and Cinnamon Sourdough Loaf Cake

*This is my favourite cake as it holds many wonderful memories. It is also very delicious served with a glass of fresh mint tea.*

- 900-g/2-lb loaf tin, lined with baking parchment, floured and buttered (do not use oil as it affects the starter)

270ml raw honey
80g fermented butter (see page 180)
150g flaked almonds

After the sourdough butter loaf cake base mix has been fermenting for 3 days, fold 120ml of the honey into the cake batter.

Bake the cake as instructed opposite, on page 156.

Meanwhile, melt the fermented butter in a pan with the remaining honey. Bring it up to a bubble, then take the pan off the heat and add the flaked almonds. Gently mix until all the almonds are coated in the honey mixture.

Once baked, remove the cake from the oven but keep the oven on.

With the cake still in the tin, spoon the honey-coated almonds over the loaf. Gently pat them down onto the top of the cake.

Return the cake to the oven and bake for a further 12 minutes or until well browned. Do not remove the cake from the tin until completely cold.

## Marrakeshi Mint and Orange Peel Sourdough Loaf Cake

*Inspired by my time living in Marrakech, this is a cake we make in summer using lots of fresh mint but with dried orange peel, which is more commonly associated with winter months.*

- 900-g/2-lb loaf tin, lined with baking parchment, floured and buttered (do not use oil as it affects the starter)

3 tablespoons finely chopped mint
1 tablespoon dried orange peel
   (available from Organic Herb Trading
   Co., or use fresh peel if you can't
   find dried)
1 tablespoon vanilla extract
25ml boiling water

**To decorate**
175g unsalted butter, softened
80g icing sugar, sifted, plus extra
   to dust
Orange peel, cut into fine strips
Handful of fresh mint leaves

Put the chopped mint and orange peel in a bowl with the vanilla extract. Pour over the boiling water and steep for 30 minutes.

After the sourdough butter loaf cake base mix has been fermenting for 3 days, fold the mint and orange peel mixture into the cake batter by hand, making sure everything is well combined.

Bake the cake as instructed on page 156.

To make the buttercream, beat together the softened butter with the icing sugar until pale and fluffy.

To decorate the cake, spoon or pipe the buttercream in a line down the top of the cake. Scatter over the strips of orange peel and then dot the mint leaves over the buttercream. Dust the cake with a little more icing sugar.

*From top to bottom:*
Marrakeshi Mint and
Orange Peel Sourdough
Loaf Cake, Morrocan
Honey and Cinnamon
Sourdough Loaf Cake.

## Date and Rosewater Sourdough Loaf Cake with Saharan Fruit Strap

*This is another of our favourite cakes at Fortitude. It's influenced by my time spent in Morocco, where they use dates in almost everything. The fruit strap came about by accident, when I had to revive some slightly overcooked dates.*

- 1 baking tray, lined with baking parchment
- 900-g/2-lb loaf tin, lined with baking parchment, floured and buttered (do not use oil as it affects the starter)

250g dried dates (the very dry, hard ones)
120ml water
1 teaspoon ground nutmeg
Rosewater jam, to glaze
Saharan fruit strap (see below),
  to decorate

**For the fruit strap**
250g dried dates
1 tablespoon rosewater
½ teaspoon ground cinnamon
80ml warm water

To make the fruit strap, place all the ingredients in a pan and simmer over a medium heat, stirring all the time, for 6 minutes or until the dates cook down to a paste. Take off the heat and make into a smooth paste by pressing the mixture through a sieve. Leave to cool completely.

Preheat the oven to 220°C/Fan 200°C/ Gas 7.

Place the fruit strap paste in the middle of a lined baking tray. Using a stepped palette knife, spread the paste as thinly as possible. Take another sheet of baking parchment and lay it on top, gently pressing down. Bake for 12 minutes or until set. Remove from the oven and leave to cool completely. Once cool, cut the paste into strips, ready to top the cake.

To make the date mixture for the cake, simmer the dates with the water for 8 minutes or until softened. Mash the dates with a fork to make a pulp. Leave to cool.

After the sourdough butter loaf cake base mix has been fermenting for 3 days, fold the date pulp into the cake batter with the ground nutmeg. Bake the cake as instructed on page 156. When the cake is cold, brush the top of the cake with rosewater jam. Drape the strips of fruit strap over the cake, arranging them however you prefer.

### Rhubarb and Lemon Sourdough Loaf Cake

*Our customers are aware of the changing food seasons, so we are always asked when rhubarb recipes will be appearing on the counter at the bakehouse. We prefer to use forced rhubarb because of its vibrant pink colour – there's always something rhubarb-y on the menu when it's available.*

- 900-g/2-lb loaf tin, lined with baking parchment, floured and buttered (do not use oil as it affects the starter)

250g forced rhubarb, cut into 2.5-cm/1-inch chunks
2 tablespoons sugar
Zest and juice of 2 organic, unwaxed lemons

Place the rhubarb pieces in a pan with the sugar and cook until soft but still keeping its shape. Leave the rhubarb to cool (this is important).

After the sourdough butter loaf cake base mix has been fermenting for 3 days, add the cooked rhubarb to the cake batter with the lemon zest and juice.

Bake the cake as instructed on page 156.

### Cold-Brew Espresso Sourdough Loaf Cake

*One day, I was planning to make a coffee and walnut cake when my daughter Sophia, who had just put some leftover cold-brew coffee in the fridge, suggested I use that rather than making a fresh shot. Now I often soak a butter cake in cold-brew coffee.*

- 900-g/2-lb loaf tin, lined with baking parchment, floured and buttered (do not use oil as it affects the starter)

200ml cold-brew coffee (see page 184)
1 tablespoon unrefined golden caster sugar
⅓ teaspoon ground cinnamon

After the sourdough butter loaf cake base mix has been fermenting for 3 days, bake the cake as instructed on page 156.

Once baked, remove the cake from the oven but keep the oven on. Leave the cake in the tin to cool for 30 minutes.

With the cake still in the tin, pour the cold-brew coffee across the top of the cake. Combine the sugar and cinnamon and sprinkle it over the loaf. Return the cake to the oven and bake for a further 10 minutes, uncovered.

*Opposite page:* Rhubarb and Lemon Sourdough Loaf Cake. For the Cold-Brew Espresso Sourdough Loaf Cake, see page 185.

# Banana *and* Bilberry Sourdough Loaf Cake

This banana loaf was the first sourdough cake I mastered; working in the heat of the Fernandez & Wells basement kitchen, it took many months of trial-and-error. Well, here is the final recipe – it works and is delicious! This cake recipe uses the buttermilk starter from page 154, but has its own fermented cake mix. Start the day before you want to bake the cake as you need to leave the batter overnight, but it can be fermented for longer. In the same way, the bananas can be fermented before being added to the batter. The mixture can be baked either as a loaf cake or as muffins. You need a deep-sided loaf tin because this cake batter will spill over the top of a shallow tin. It's also a very bready mixture and so needs the shape.

**Makes 1 loaf cake or
12 muffins**

• 900-g/2-lb loaf tin, lined
   with baking parchment,
   floured and buttered
   (do not use oil as it affects
   the starter)

4 small, very ripe bananas
185g light muscovado sugar
3 eggs
90ml buttermilk (see
   page 180)
70ml pomace oil
   (or light virgin olive oil)
180g organic plain white flour
2 teaspoons ground cinnamon
80g buttermilk starter (see
   page 154) with 1 teaspoon
   bicarbonate of soda folded
   in gently
120g bilberries (blueberries
   work too or use any other
   soft fruits you have around)

In a bowl, mash the bananas with a fork until almost liquid. Place the sugar and eggs into the bowl of a mixer and beat on medium speed until just combined. Add the buttermilk and oil, then the mashed bananas. Add the flour and ground cinnamon and mix well for 2 minutes. Finally, fold in the buttermilk starter using your hands. Pour the cake batter into a bowl and cover with a clean tea towel. Leave overnight at room temperature.

Preheat the oven to 200°C/Fan 180°C/Gas 6.

When ready to bake, fold the bilberries or other soft fruits into the cake batter. Pour the cake batter into the lined and greased loaf tin or muffin moulds. Bake for 45 minutes for a loaf cake and 25 minutes for muffins. Test the loaf cake by inserting a skewer and checking that it comes out clean – the cake rises beautifully but can fool you into thinking that it's done, so always check. Leave the cake in the tin to cool.

When stored in an airtight container in the fridge, this loaf cake will keep for 7 days.

TO FERMENT
The cake batter can be fermented, which I really recommend. After leaving it overnight at room

temperature (which kickstarts the process), cover and rest in the fridge for up to 7 days. The mashed bananas can also be fermented before being added to the cake batter. Place them in a sealed container and store them at room temperature for up to 7 days.

# Guinness *and* Chocolate Fermented Loaf

I have been making this dense chocolate cake for many years. In fact, I remember attempting it with my sister for a Home Economics bake sale while still at school. It was a bit of a disaster, but we were on the right track. You'll need to leave the mixture overnight before baking.

**Makes 1 loaf cake or**
**1 round cake**

- 900-g/2-lb loaf tin or 23-cm/9-inch round springform tin, lined with baking parchment

225ml Guinness (or other dark Irish stout)
350g dark muscovado sugar
225g fermented butter (see page 178)
300g organic plain wholemeal flour
65g good-quality cocoa powder, plus extra to dust
3 eggs
175g live natural yogurt
60g buttermilk starter (see page 154) with 1 teaspoon bicarbonate of soda folded in

**For the buttercream**
175g salted butter, softened
80g icing sugar, sifted

Place the Guinness, sugar and fermented butter in a pan and heat gently, stirring, until the sugar has dissolved. Remove from the heat and leave to cool. Once cool, transfer to a large mixing bowl.

Sift together the flour and cocoa in a bowl. In a separate bowl, beat the eggs with the yogurt. Add the egg and yogurt mixture to the flour, stirring to combine.

Add that flour mixture to the cooled Guinness mixture. Leave for 10 minutes so it is completely cold, then fold in the buttermilk starter using your hands. Cover and leave in the fridge overnight or for 2 days if you have time.

Preheat the oven to 200°C/Fan 180°C/Gas 6.

Pour the cake batter into the lined tin and bake for 55 minutes or until a skewer inserted into the centre comes out clean. Leave the cake in the tin to cool.

Meanwhile, make the buttercream. Place the butter and sugar in the bowl of a mixer and beat with a paddle attachment on high speed for 3 minutes or until creamed. Spoon the buttercream over the top of the cake, creating swirls with the back of the spoon. Dust with extra cocoa.

When stored in an airtight container in the fridge, this cake keeps for up to 5 days.

TO FERMENT
Leave the cake batter to ferment in the fridge up to 2 for days, but no longer – it doesn't need a long ferment as it's really powerful.

# Spanish Fermented Butter Cake *with* Fizzy Apricots

I wrote this recipe for my partner Jorge. It uses fermented butter to recreate the unique taste of the cake he remembers eating as a kid – it's what makes this cake stand out. Served with clotted cream, it becomes an amazing dessert. The fizzy apricots can be served with all sorts of things and the boozy syrup from the jar is wonderful chilled.

**Makes 1 loaf cake**

- 900-g/2-lb loaf tin, lined with baking parchment, floured and buttered (do not use oil as it affects the starter)

300g fermented butter (see page 178), softened
200g soft light brown sugar
4 eggs
225g organic plain white flour
50g ground almonds
150g buttermilk starter (see page 154)
150g fizzy apricots or 100g fizzy cherries (see page 183), finely chopped
150ml fizzy apricots or cherry preserving syrup (see page 183)
Icing sugar, to dust

Preheat the oven to 200°C/Fan 180°C/Gas 6.

Place 200g of the fermented butter and the sugar in the bowl of a mixer fitted with a paddle attachment and beat on medium speed for 5 minutes or until light and creamy. Add the eggs one at a time, mixing between each addition.

Reduce the speed of the mixer to slow and add the flour and ground almonds in three batches, making sure everything is well combined.

Fold in the buttermilk starter using your hands. Finally, add the fizzy apricots or fizzy cherries.

Pour the cake batter into the prepared tin and bake for 1 hour 15 minutes or until a skewer inserted into the centre of the cake comes out clean.

Meanwhile, warm the remaining fermented butter with the fizzy preserving syrup in a pan over a high heat until it starts to bubble.

Once baked, remove the cake from the oven but keep the oven on. With the cake still in the tin, pour the buttery syrup over the loaf. Return the cake to the oven and bake for a further 8 minutes or until well browned. Do not remove the cake from the tin until completely cold, then dust with icing sugar.

When stored in an airtight container in the fridge, this cake keeps for 7 days.

# Fermented Tea
# Spelt Fruit Cake

We regularly make kombucha at the bakery, which inspired me to use fermented tea in a fruit cake to give it some fizz and a bit of tang. We make the tea and leave it in a preserving jar for five days. I also soak the fruit for up to three days beforehand, but overnight is fine too. This is a pudding-like cake that can be heated up in slices and eaten with custard, like a bread pudding. This cake also happens to be vegan.

**Makes 1 round cake**

• 2-litre preserving jar and
  20-cm/8-inch round tin,
  lined with baking parchment

**For the fermented tea**

3 tablespoons any strong,
  dark loose-leaf tea
2 litres boiling water
2 tablespoons unrefined
  golden caster sugar

**For the cake**

200g raisins
200g sultanas
100g currants
100g mixed orange peel
500ml fermented tea
  (not the mother)
355g organic wholemeal
  spelt flour
½ teaspoon ground cloves
½ teaspoon ground mace
100g buttermilk starter (see
  page 154) with 1 teaspoon
  bicarbonate of soda folded in
4 tablespoons black treacle

To make the fermented tea, place the tea leaves in a heatproof bowl and pour over the boiling water. Leave the tea to brew for 1 hour.

Pass the brewed tea through a sieve into the preserving jar. Add the caster sugar. Leave in a cool, dry place for 5 days. You will see that the tea starts to create a mother at the bottom of the jar, which is a good thing. (This can be kept to make a mother for kombucha.)

To make the cake, place the dried fruit and peel in a bowl. Pour over 500ml of fermented tea from the jar (avoiding the mother). Cover and leave to soak at room temperature overnight or for up to 3 days, if you have time.

Preheat the oven to 180°C/Fan 160°C/Gas 5.

Combine the flour and spices in a bowl. Add the flour to the bowl with the tea-soaked fruit and then fold in the buttermilk starter. Finally, stir in the black treacle.

Pour the cake batter into the tin and smooth over the top. Bake for 2 hours or until it springs back to the touch. Halfway through the cooking time, lay a disc of baking parchment over the top of the cake. To check the cake is cooked, insert a skewer into the centre – if it comes out clean, the cake is done. Leave in the tin to cool.

When stored in an airtight container in the fridge, this cake will keep for up to 2 weeks. It will gain more of a tang by the end of the second week.

# Fermented Carrot
# *and* Kefir Cake

This is our go-to birthday cake recipe. We use a lot of the vegetables and fruit that the greengrocer cannot sell to his other customers because they are misshapen. It's a crime to throw away lovely produce that we can happily use in our bakes. We peel and grate wonky carrots and leave them to ferment in jars in the fridge for a week, after which time they become very wet and develop a sweet, slightly fermented taste that is perfect in our carrot and kefir cake. In this recipe, the carrots are soaked with the sultanas in kefir overnight.

**Makes 1 sandwiched cake**

- 2 × 23-cm/9-inch round
  springform cake tins, lined
  with baking parchment

250g carrots (about 4 medium
  carrots), peeled, grated and
  stored in a jar in the fridge
  for 7 days to ferment
60g sultanas
120ml kefir milk
275g organic plain wholemeal
  flour
1 teaspoon ground cinnamon
½ teaspoon ground nutmeg
½ teaspoon dried orange peel
  (available from Organic Herb
  Trading Co.)
280ml pomace oil (or light
  virgin olive oil)
400g dark muscovado sugar
5 eggs
65g buttermilk starter (see
  page 154) with 2 teaspoons
  bicarbonate of soda folded in
100g shelled walnuts,
  chopped

Put the fermented carrot and sultanas in a bowl. Pour over the kefir milk and leave in the fridge overnight.

The next day, combine the flour, spices and dried orange peel in a bowl.

Whisk together the pomace oil and sugar until combined, then add the eggs one at a time, making sure that each one is well combined.

Fold in the flour mixture in three batches until well combined. Fold in the buttermilk starter. Finally fold in the carrot, sultana and kefir mix. Cover with a clean tea towel and leave to rest for 1 hour.

When ready to bake, preheat the oven to 220°C/Fan 200°C/Gas 7.

Fold the chopped walnuts into the batter and then divide it between the two lined cake tins. Bake for 45 minutes or until it springs back to the touch. Leave the cakes in the tins to cool.

Meanwhile, make the topping. Whisk the icing sugar and cream cheese together with the hot water until light and fluffy, then fold in the whipped double cream.

When completely cold, remove the cakes from the tins and spread a thin layer of the topping over one cake.

**For the topping**

150g icing sugar

250g cream cheese

1 tablespoon hot water

85ml double cream,
 whipped

**To decorate**

Candied fruits

Orange peel curls

Rosemary sprigs

Mint leaves

Pumpkin seeds

Place the second cake on top of the first to make a sandwich. Dollop the rest of the topping onto the cake, spreading it as you like with the back of a spoon or a palette knife.

Decorate the top of the cake by arranging candied fruits and orange peel curls in a crescent shape. Dot with small rosemary sprigs and mint leaves, then scatter over a few pumpkin seeds.

When stored in an airtight container in the fridge, this cake will keep for 7 days.

# Store-
cupboard

This chapter is all about refining the craft of baking. Of course, you can buy perfectly good versions of these preserves, spice mixes and dairy products, but if you want to make everything from scratch then these recipes are really straightforward – plus they are enjoyable to make.

The good thing about making your own storecupboard staples is that you can adjust them to your taste. My spice mixes tend to be very balanced, but you can add more or less of one spice to suit your own taste or purpose. With spice mixes, I hate to disagree with those who say it doesn't matter if your spices are a bit old, but it does make a difference – if one spice is stronger than another, it will dominate and so throw the balance off. In Morocco, when a spice has lost its flavour, it is considered 'dead'. However, you can use these dead spices to flavour sugar, even dried ones like lavender, orange or oregano – the moisture in the grains of sugar will revive the spice.

The dairy recipes are really more for the cold store than storecupboard, but fermented butter, labneh and ricotta all play an important part in my baking. They bring the depth and complexity of flavour that I always talk about. Buttermilk is especially easy to make at home too.

I don't like to waste anything in the kitchen. There is always a way to use up ingredients. The salty-sweet preserved lemons are different from the traditional salt-preserved lemons, but you can also dry orange peel, or lemon or lime. When we use oranges for juicing, first we take off the peel and cook it in orange syrup to slice it thinly to top cakes with – like candied fruit, it brings colour to cake decoration. When we have excess fruit like cherries, we preserve them in syrup following the recipe for fizzy apricots.

I made the honey marzipan (see page 184) first at Bumblebee as a way to replace sugar – the honey also means that the marzipan is less crunchy. I also make a vegan version with agar agar, almonds and spices.

For those new to baking or who feel it's all a bit of a faff, once you've gained confidence from making a recipe a few times, I really recommend taking it a step further by making the accompanying storecupboard recipe rather than using shop-bought versions. Not only will you taste the difference it makes, but you will also feel like a true craft baker.

# Ras el Hanout

Ras el hanout means 'top of the shop' in Arabic. You will find that every Moroccan family has their choice of spices and each spice seller in the souk will also have their recommendations. This is my choice. Always make sure that your spices are fresh.

**Makes 1 small jar**

2 tablespoons ground
  cinnamon
1 tablespoon ground cumin
1 tablespoon ground nutmeg
1 teaspoon ground ginger
1 teaspoon chilli powder
1 teaspoon ground coriander

Place all the ingredients in a jar and shake vigorously.

When stored in an airtight jar in a cool place, this spice mix will last for 8 weeks.

# Za'atar

My spice mixes tend to be very balanced. Some like their za'atar with a strong taste of mountain thyme, so that it's herby rather than sesame seedy. I prefer to use equal quantities here. I use fresh thyme which makes my za'atar really fragrant.

**Makes 1 small jar**

4 tablespoons fresh or
  dried thyme
4 tablespoons toasted
  sesame seeds
3 teaspoons ground sumac
1 teaspoon fine sea salt
1 teaspoon dried oregano
½ teaspoon ground black
  pepper

Place all the ingredients in a jar and shake vigorously.

When stored in an airtight jar in a cool place, this spice mix will last for 8 weeks.

Traditionally the pain d'épices is made with a mix of five spices, but they vary from baker to baker. This one is mine.

**Makes 1 small jar**

Place all the ingredients in a jar and shake vigorously.

1 tablespoon ground cinnamon
1 tablespoon ground ginger
1 tablespoon ground nutmeg
½ teaspoon ground cloves
½ teaspoon ground mace

When stored in an airtight jar in a cool place, this spice mix will last for 8 weeks.

# Chilli Sugar

This flavoured sugar is really nice in biscuits, especially a sablé or the Arabic almond biscuits, ghoraibi.

**Makes 1 large jar**

Place both the ingredients in a jar and shake vigorously.

400g unrefined golden
  caster sugar
1 tablespoon chilli powder

When stored in an airtight jar a cool place, this flavoured sugar will last for 8 weeks.

# Fermented Butter

I make fermented or cultured butter often for events at the bakery or for a one-off cake request. It's a simple process and the finished butter tastes wonderful spread on wholemeal soda bread with sea salt. I also use it in my Spanish fermented butter cake (see page 168).

**Makes 1 litre**

1 litre double cream
250g live natural yogurt
2 tablespoons fine sea salt

In a bowl, whisk together the cream and yogurt by hand for 3 minutes. Cover with a cheesecloth and leave out of the fridge, at room temperature, for 24 hours. After 24 hours, chill in the fridge for 2 hours.

Transfer the butter to a mixer fitted with a whisk attachment and whisk initially on the slow setting for 2 minutes, then increase to high speed – you will see that the fat starts to separate and thicken. This takes about 5 minutes.

Wrap the thickened butter in muslin and squeeze tightly to drain off any excess liquid (keep the excess liquid for adding to your soda bread).

Work the salt through with a wooden spoon, then roll the butter into two logs and wrap it in wax paper.

When stored in the fridge, this butter will keep for up to 2 weeks. When you need to use it, bring it back to room temperature for 2 hours.

# Buttermilk

Buttermilk is highly acidic. When combined with bicarbonate of soda, it creates a wonderful reaction that gives a good rise to bakes as well as a slight tang to the taste. The acid in the milk helps to tenderise gluten which gives soda breads a lovely soft texture. Buttermilk is so simple to make – just add a tablespoon of lemon juice for every 250ml of milk.

**Makes 1 litre**

1 litre full-fat milk, at room
   temperature
4 tablespoons lemon juice
   or white wine vinegar

Add the lemon juice to the milk. The milk will start to curdle, but that's what you are looking for. It curdles really quickly, within an hour but often quicker, at room temperature.

When stored in a sealed jar in the fridge, this buttermilk will keep for 3 days.

# Labneh

I have been making labneh for many years – I use it in cakes, in salads or as a dip. In Morocco it is eaten with fig jam (see page 183) or with a type of za'atar, chopped fresh mint and plenty of olive oil. The thickness of the final labneh is determined by two things – how runny your yogurt is and how long you strain it for.

**Makes about 500g**

1kg live natural yogurt
   (I use the mid-runny type
   from Northiam Dairy)
2 tablespoons fine sea salt

Line a large sieve with cheesecloth and place it over a glass bowl to catch the whey. (I use the whey in soda bread as I don't like to waste it.) Combine the yogurt and salt, then pour the mixture into the cheesecloth. I always place a heavy plate with a folded tea towel on top to add a little pressure.

Leave for 12–24 hours in a cool place but not in the fridge. The longer you leave it the thicker the labneh will be.

Once made, the labneh can be stored in the fridge. Follow the 'use-by' date on your yogurt.

Every January, when the Seville oranges came into season, my mum used to make this marmalade. I would sit beside her and make the marmalade with her. She always warmed the sugar first, before it became known – my mother really understood the process and her marmalade was always beautiful.

**Makes about 2.5kg**

1.75kg Seville oranges
2 litres water
Juice of 4 lemons
2.5kg granulated sugar

Scrub the oranges until clean, place in a large pan and cover with the water. Bring to the boil, cover and simmer for 2 hours until the oranges are soft. Remove the oranges from the pan and leave to cool, keeping the pan with the cooking liquid to one side.

Preheat the oven to 160°C/Fan 140°C/Gas 3.

Spread the sugar over a baking tray and warm in the oven for 10 minutes – this helps the jam to set.

Scoop all the flesh, pith and seeds out of the oranges and place in a cheesecloth. Squeeze the juice through the cheesecloth back into the pan of the orange cooking water. Add the warmed sugar to the pan and bring it to the boil.

Cut the orange skins into fine strips, place in the orange water and continue to bubble until it reaches the setting point of 105°C on a jam thermometer.

Divide the marmalade between warmed sterilised jars in whatever shapes or sizes you have available.

# Sweet and Salty
# Preserved Lemons

We use these preserved lemons in our cakes but also in our salads, as a garnish for our cold soups and in stews with chickpeas and mint. I make these whenever I can get hold of good organic, unwaxed lemons. I have three jars of these sweet and sour lemons in the bakery, which are now three years old – and they still taste exceptional.

**Fills a 1.2-litre/2-pint preserving jar**

150g fine sea salt
150g unrefined golden caster
  sugar
1kg unwaxed lemons, washed
Filtered water

Combine the salt and sugar in a bowl. Cut the lemons lengthways almost down to the base but not all the way through, leaving 1cm/½ inch uncut at the bottom. Stuff each lemon with the salt and sugar mixture.

Pack the lemons tightly into the preserving jar or another sealable vessel. Fill with filtered water until it reaches the top of the jar, then pack any remaining salt and sugar mixture on top. Seal the jar tightly and store in a cool place, but not in the fridge. Do not even think of opening the jar and trying the lemons for at least 6 weeks.

# Fig Jam

During a visit to Morocco, I stayed at a place in the High Atlas where they served Moroccan bread with goat's cheese, sweet tomato jam and a delicious fig jam. I thought to myself, I'm definitely making that when I get home. You can slice the figs into quarters if you want, but I leave them because I like to see the whole fig in a jam.

**Makes about 1kg**

1.5kg figs, either left whole or
   cut into quarters
Juice of 2 lemons
500g granulated sugar
½ teaspoon ground nutmeg
250ml warm water

Place all the ingredients in a heavy-based saucepan and bring up to a bubble. Reduce the heat and simmer for 15 minutes until the jam has reduced by a quarter and is now thick.

Divide the jam between warmed sterilised jars in whatever shapes or sizes you have available.

## Fizzy Apricots and Cherries

I learned quickly that these fizzy apricots can explode into a sticky mess if not refrigerated. We also realised that the syrup makes a really nice base for champagne cocktails.

**Makes 1 large jar**

1kg fresh apricots and/or
   fresh cherries, washed
   and stoned
1 litre water
500g unrefined golden
   caster sugar

Place the washed and stoned fruit in a preserving jar.

To make a sugar syrup, bring the water and sugar to the boil in a pan. Remove the pan from the heat and leave to cool.

Pour the sugar syrup over the fruit, seal the jar and place it in the fridge for 6 weeks.

# Honey Marzipan

As lots of my customers at Bumblebee didn't like sugary marzipan, I made this honeyed alternative to top Christmas cakes and Simnel cakes. At Fortitude, we use it in our cinnamon brioche (see page 147).

**Makes 700g**

450g ground almonds
2 tablespoons orange
  flower water
250g raw honey
2 teaspoons icing sugar

Place the ground almonds, orange flower water and honey in the bowl of a mixer fitted with a paddle attachment. Beat together on medium speed for 2 minutes or until everything is well combined.

Transfer the marzipan from the bowl to a clean surface lightly dusted with icing sugar. Gently knead the marzipan and then roll into a log. Cover in food wrap.

When stored in an airtight container in the fridge, this marzipan will keep for up to 6 weeks.

# Cold-Brew Coffee

This is an infusion rather than a ferment because, if left for more than 12 hours, the coffee becomes bitter. This is wonderful drunk over ice.

**Makes 900ml**

130g whole coffee beans
900ml cold filtered water

Grind the coffee beans on a coarse setting. Combine the ground coffee and the water in a preserving jar and stir well, making sure everything is thoroughly combined. Seal the jar and leave in a cool place for 12 hours.

Strain the contents of the preserving jar through a muslin or cheesecloth into another clean jar and seal.

When stored in a sealed jar in the fridge, this coffee will keep for up to 7 days.

A huge thank you to Bloomsbury Publishing for seeing something in me that I don't always see in myself. Special thanks to Lisa Pendreigh, who instantly recognised our craft and always enjoys our bakes, and also to Kitty Stogdon, who kept me on the straight and narrow while writing this book. Thanks too to Rowan Yapp for her support and Jonathan Hayden, my literary agent, who has over the years pushed me in the right direction.

Thanks to the super-talented Laura Edwards, who photographed this book so beautifully, ably assisted by the lovely Jo Cowan, whose hands can be seen throughout the book. Laura made the shoot incredibly special with her patience and gave me the confidence to style my bakes as I would want. And to Charlotte Heal, a talented designer who translated our vision brilliantly.

I cannot thank my co-writer Muna Reyal, multi-talented editor, enough. Muna listened and interpreted my words with an ear that astounds me. She heard my voice and understood my devotion to a craft I have managed to sustain for over twenty years. She pushed me when I needed it, with lots of gentle nudges towards deadlines, even when I had 4am starts. Thank you, my friend.

Thanks to my wonderful family, who are as devoted to me as I am to them. To Rachid, who has believed in me and encouraged me throughout our lives. To Soumiya, Sophia and Zakiyy, my children and the loves of my life, who have grown up in many kitchens and bakeries and have always had complete understanding of my need to keep working. They are, in their own right, three of the most talented and individual human beings I have ever met. To my parents, grandparents and siblings, who enabled me to think I could actually be successful in kitchens at a time when women were not always easily accepted. I inherited the strong woman backbone from these stoic people, and they have provided the knowledge, the sustenance and the provenance that have enabled me to have a career that I love.

To all who work and have worked at Fortitude, thank you for your hard work and commitment. And to all the folks I have worked with over the years. Each one of you brought a story or a drama to the table; life was never boring in our kitchens, you know who you are!

Most of all, thank you to the wonderful Jorge, the man with much Fortitude.